Winds of Grace

A Memoir of Losing my Father, Surrendering Control, and Growing in Faith

Cheryl Esper Balcom

Cheryl Balcom
2 Cor. 12:9

Winds of Grace

A Memoir of Losing my Father, Surrendering Control, and Growing in Faith

The events and conversations in this book have been set down to the best of the author's ability, although some details and names have been changed or omitted to protect the privacy of individuals.

Cover photo courtesy of the Esper family
To view more photos from this story, visit the author's website at www.cherylesperbalcom.com

Cover design by 100Covers.com

Author photo by Shannon McDonald Photography

Paperback ISBN: 979-8-9872207-0-2

eBook ISBN: 979-8-9872207-1-9

For Mom

For getting on the boat though you couldn't swim,
and for showing me how to hold onto God's hand.

and in memory of Dad

You are my sunshine
and because of you,
the Lord is my light.
Thank you.

And for you, my reader friend.

Thank you for reading these words.
I pray that the Lord uses them to fill
your heart with a fresh reminder
of His grace for you, and a longing to know Him more.
He will not disappoint.

Table of Contents

Chapter 1 1
Chapter 2 9
Chapter 3 25
Chapter 4 45
Chapter 5 55
Chapter 6 63
Chapter 7 73
Chapter 8 91
Chapter 9 109
Chapter 10 117
Chapter 11 125
Chapter 12 137
Chapter 13 155
Epilogue 169
Appendix 173
About the Author 183

Prologue

On October 14, 2005, I write four sentences in my prayer journal:

My dad has cancer.
Father, hold him in your hands right now.
Oh Lord, help us to take one day at a time.
Your grace is sufficient.

The words are so heavy I can barely lift my pen to write them. But this phrase is one that I love, this one about grace.

"My grace is sufficient for you, for my power is made perfect in weakness." (2 Corinthians 12:9)

The Bible verse flows from my tongue easily and automatically when times are difficult and I feel weak.

But what is grace, really? How can something that I cannot touch or handle be strong? How can it be enough for me? I conjure up what *sufficient* looks like in my mind, and I see cement foundations and paved roads and boulders, strong things, solid to stand on. How can a word that evokes images of ballet, a word that rhymes with *lace* for crying out loud, be enough for me in this moment? How can grace be sufficient when what I want are answers, miracles?

How can it be enough if it requires nothing from me?

Chapter 1

The Lord is the portion of my inheritance and my cup;
You support my lot.
The lines have fallen to me in pleasant places;
Indeed, my heritage is beautiful to me.

Psalm 16:5 NASB

Summer 2005

The clear, blue water of Torch Lake glittered in the sunlight. Shouts of laughter carried across the water from my brother-in-law's boat as he pulled everyone in turn on the tube behind it. The smaller kids, bedecked in inflatable wings and inner tubes, played in the crystalline water near the shore as they filled buckets and built sandcastles under my mother's watchful eye.

The afternoon was gloriously sunny, painting us red and building up our reserves of vitamin D to help us endure the next Michigan winter. My dad sat in the shade between two strollers that held his infant grandsons, my nephews, Elijah and Sam. The three of them napped in the warm breeze while Jim and I ate lunch at the picnic table before heading back into the water.

After living in Otsego, a town just south of Grand Rapids, Michigan, for 27 years and raising their family, Mom and Dad had said goodbye to the house just last week, kissing the front door while holding hands. They waved to the semi-trailer that carried their possessions to a storage unit in Zeeland, where their new condo was being built; their sailboat waited for them in a slip on Lake Macatawa a few miles away. While my parents lived out of suitcases and waited with anticipation for the next chapter of their life to begin, three of us kids and our families vacationed with them in a rental cabin on Torch River.

In his sloppy handwriting, Dad chronicled our adventures that week on a yellow legal pad, titling it, "A Brief Review of 'Cabin Week' Vacation." Affection for his kids and grandkids oozed onto the page as he detailed who was there and what events took place each day. Everything from the weather to what we had for dinner, who almost got lost in the woods to who caught how many fish (and the stats of each catch) was recorded with enthusiasm. That day was Friday: "Cool day, sunny and bright – swim, tube at Torch Lake Township Park from 1:00 p.m. to 7:00 – lunch on the grill."

We took two full days to celebrate Dad's 60th birthday a year ago. He thought only the kids and grandkids were coming, but Mom surprised him by inviting about fifty friends and family to celebrate under party tents in the big backyard. The following day was spent with just the family, sailing and picnicking at Gull Lake. Both days were sunny and filled with laughter, softball, swimming, sailing, fantastic food, and plenty of toasts "to Frankie!"

A few weeks ago, the marking of his 61st birthday was a quiet evening on the deck by the pool, the final family gathering at the blue house on 108th Avenue.

Now I sit back on my towel on the beach, burying my feet in the warm sand and soaking in the sunshine. I am 35, and my life is pleasantly full; our four kids are 10, 7, 4, and 3, and it feels so good to be here, to be on vacation. It feels so good to have family that are becoming my best friends.

I silently thank the Lord for my parents, for the excitement of their upcoming move; I thank Him for my healthy kids and my sweet husband and for the time to get away to the cabin and have fun together. And I thank Him for my upbringing, for giving me parents who love Him and love each other; for a dad who has always reminded us, "The best thing I can do for you kids is love your mother."

I thank God for the power of laughter that helps us survive family drama, and I thank Him for grace because I know none of it is deserved. I did nothing to earn any of these blessings; so, like the rays of sun on my shoulders, I soak them in.

My family wasn't perfect, by any means. We were blessed to have two parents who loved each other and were committed to staying married. There were seven of us kids, depending on which year you counted. Four of us were born to Frank and Lynda; three more were folded in through adoption before any of us were teenagers. Things got sticky for a while; we were a blended family without the stepparents. We had magical times and we had times of heartbreak. There was chaos, there were cracks, but there was also laughter; so much so that at times we ached from it. We stumbled over each other as we tried to make our way but even in the darkest of times, the Lord was present and my parents pursued Him.

1992 was a big year. I, the oldest of the bunch, married my college sweetheart, Jim, and moved to Michigan's Upper Peninsula. My sister Reneé, a nineteen-year-old single mom, had moved herself and her baby into an apartment and was attending a local university. My two brothers both left for school: one to college and the other, who needed space and structure, to a private high school on the east side of the state. That left three sisters in high school at home, and for the first time in twenty-three years, my mom took a part-time job outside of the home.

The Esper nest was emptying in a ruffle of wedding lace, diapers, and tuition payments. Determined to keep us all connected wherever we landed, my parents decided to invest in a time share at a ski and golf resort in northern Michigan. My dad was never an avid golfer, though he would play for fun with friends; my mom neither skied nor golfed. They just loved it up there, plain and simple. The quaint, village-like feel of the resort–dotted with cozy cottages, inns, and townhouses nestled against a snow-covered ski hill–would provide the perfect backdrop for quiet get-aways and extended family times together. 1992 would begin a 30-plus year tradition of Thanksgivings at Crystal Mountain

By Thanksgiving of 1999, Jim and I had two kids, ages four and two; the two-year-old was just starting to manifest some of the challenges of her Williams Syndrome diagnosis, a genetic disorder discovered when she was a baby.

Reneé was there with her new husband; her son Tyler was turning ten that weekend, and we would celebrate not just his birthday but a decade of life that had brought joy from crisis. My brother Simeon and sisters Kelly and Miriam were single young adults seeking to mark their place in the world.

There were still some cracks in the family; one adopted sibling was estranged, another living out west and just beginning to renew connections with the family after a period of separation.

We were a hodge-podge group of flawed yet striving humans still in the early stages of recognizing the gift of family, and that year Mom and Dad traded their rental time for a larger space at Crystal: a townhouse with a full kitchen where we could prepare our Thanksgiving dinner together.

Before the meal, Dad stood before us, his plaid shirt wet at the belly from doing dishes and a thoughtfully scribbled prayer in his hand.

Recently, I had begun to observe a pattern in men as they grew older. It was a softening of the years, a sentimental smoothing of rough edges. A tenderness when it came to family. I saw it starting to emerge in my dad as his voice quivered–just a little–as he began his prayer. He cleared his throat and swiped his graying hair off his forehead before he continued:

Today is Thanksgiving.
Lord God Almighty
Creator of all things
Giver of life,
Today we give you special thanks.
Thanks for the simple things you give us –
Food, shelter, warmth;
Thanks for the special things you give us –
A loving family, acceptance, patience, and understanding.
Thank you, Lord, for the things we take for granted:
Our health
Our wealth
Our abilities
Each other.
America, our country.
Thank you, Lord,
For all the families we are becoming –
Espers and Yakes and Balcoms ... and more to come...
Thank you, especially Lord, for the everlasting things –
The things not seen which endure forever:
Forgiveness
Wisdom
Your love
Hope
Grace
Salvation.
We pray for and thank you for

the continuation of this family –
For Tyler
For Jared
For Courtney
And for the children not yet born
to the people around this table.
May we all be faithful to you, Jesus,
In how we live
And in what we do and say,
What we teach in word and by example
To our children and children's children
And for eternity.
Amen

The cabin at Torch River was lively and full ("Balcoms: six, Yakes: five, Ashbys: three, and Frank and Lynda, two," Dad recorded), and the evenings had been filled with fishing off the dock, canoe rides on the river, grilling our dinner and playing card games, Wizard being the current family favorite.

Dad seemed tired by the end of the week, but I knew he and Mom were both distracted by the upcoming move. It had been a jam-packed slew of active, hot days ("Tuesday: 90 degrees; the whole gang sat in the river.") On our last night, Dad was wiped out and declined to play one last game of Wizard with us at the table; he lay quietly on the couch and read instead.

Not far in the future, I would look back on this vacation and realize that God was moving during that week in the cabin. He was giving gifts of time and memories, providing something to savor in the months to come.

Chapter 2

Where my parents dwelt,
home was rich and heaven was close.

-Sarah Clarkson

September 1973

In a little yellow house in Kalamazoo, Michigan, I stood on my tiptoes to reach up and touch the face of my new baby brother. Reneé stood next to me in matching footie pajamas as Mom lowered the baby toward us carefully, reminding us to be gentle. His head was fuzzy and his face was wrinkled, like the grizzled old man from the Bible he was named for.

Later that night, Mom rocked baby Simeon to the sound of a strummed guitar in the living room. Friends of my parents sat in a circle on the floor and, as I lay on my stomach in my bed, I could hear them singing songs of praise to God. While Reneé sucked her two fingers in the twin bed across from me, I self-soothed by lifting one leg at the knee and then letting it drop on my lime-green comforter, over and over until my eyes grew heavy. I fell asleep to the soft sounds of worship.

Make a joyful noise unto the Lord,
All ye, all ye lands
Serve the Lord, the Lord with gladness
Come before His presence with singing.
Glory glory, Glory hallelujah
Glory glory, Glory hallelujah

2002

On a carefully saved, greasy Pizza Hut napkin I had a timeline of my parents' history, written in my dad's handwriting. One night during my pregnancy with Audrey, I craved melted mozzarella cheese, so we met my parents for dinner. While the kids ate pizza, drank root beer, and put quarters in the jukebox, Dad answered my curious questions about the timeline of their life together. He provided a visual framework as he was often known to do–especially on restaurant napkins.

From East Detroit and Dearborn and raised in the Catholic church, my parents were both younger children of large families and born in the mid-1940s. My dad was the fourth of five boys, my mom the youngest of six children. Dad was adventurous, almost impulsive; with so many brothers, he was raised with mischief. He loved to learn new things and was an active and hands-on kid, while Mom was more reserved, somewhat shy but creative.

Dad read aloud as he wrote on the napkin:

"1963-Dad meets Mom. 1964-Mom dumps Dad."

We looked at each other and burst out laughing.

As he continued to write in dates, he explained that he had graduated from Orchard Lake St. Mary's Preparatory high school in '62; Mom finished school at East Detroit High two years later. Dad attended–and eventually dropped out of–Eastern Michigan University, deciding to enlist in the Air Force in 1966.

After completing basic training, he was stationed at Luke Air Force base in Arizona, where he applied for the Officer Candidate program. Dad then chose to attend Auburn University to finish his bachelor's degree; from there he made the long drive back to Michigan in 1967 to be the best man in the wedding of a close friend. This particular couple happened to be the ones who had introduced him to Mom years earlier; lo and behold, she was the maid of honor at this very wedding.

Mom had worked part-time as a legal secretary for a local law firm during and after high school, saving her money to buy her first sewing machine. She was inspired to learn to sew by her older brother's wife and took a class in high school. She sewed for people from home for a while, doing alterations and making dresses and skirts. These skills helped her to get a job at J.L. Hudson's Department Store doing alterations.

But Mom, who had joined the Young Democrats in 1965, soon found herself working on the campaign for John Bruff, who was running for Michigan's lieutenant governor. She caught the attention of Congressman James O'Hara, who wanted someone from his home district working for him in Washington, so Mom moved to D.C. in '66. After reconnecting with Dad at Bill and Mary Lou's wedding, they began to date long-distance, and the rest is history.

When we were kids, Dad famously would tell the story of how, when he proposed to my mom after an Auburn football game, he reverently bent down on one knee and asked her tenderly, "Lynda? Will you be my wife and the mother of my children?" According to Dad, she immediately said, (here Dad would raise his voice to a high, southern hillbilly drawl) "Wha shaw, Frankie!" making us kids giggle every time at this contrary picture of our mother.

After their marriage in Detroit in June 1968, Dad and Mom loaded up their belongings in–and on top of–their red Volkswagen Beetle and began the long, marriage-building drive back to Alabama so Dad could finish his degree at Auburn.

After Dad completed his Officer Training School in Texas during the summer after their wedding, my parents followed Hurricane Camille to Biloxi, Mississippi, in the fall of '69. They made a cozy home for themselves near Keesler Air Force Base, where I was born that November.

My sister Reneé was born in January 1971 while my parents were stationed in Panama. As the Vietnam War began to die down, Dad was discharged from the Air Force and they began to think about moving back to Michigan.

Drawing a circle on the other side of the napkin at Pizza Hut, Dad explained to me, "So, here's Detroit." He scribbled a little star in the middle of the circle. "Your mom and I discussed how we wanted to live within a maximum 300 -mile radius"–here he drew lines that protruded from the star–"from our families in Detroit. Well, your Aunt Judy and Uncle Jerry already lived in Otsego, on the west side of the state, so we moved to Kalamazoo when I took the job at Parker. Your Grandma Esper loaned us a thousand dollars as a down payment to buy the house on Starlite."

Dad took the job with Parker-Hannifin as an industrial engineer to support his little family, and Mom stayed home to care for us. While living in Panama, my parents had begun a Christ-centered, Bible-based home fellowship that was modeled after the gatherings my Aunt Diane and Uncle Harry were involved in in the Detroit area. Mom and Dad continued this after moving back to the States.

The Jesus Movement was in full swing then, carrying into the 1970s this new, earthy enthusiasm for authentic worship and care for others. Jesus had become a big deal, the Main Thing, to my parents and, though their upbringing had provided a firm foundation for their faith, they desired to cleave to Christ and listen more closely to the Holy Spirit.

In my memories of this little house, I see Dad waking up one night and scaring himself when he saw his reflection in the hallway mirror, a story often repeated with laughter. I feel his arms catching my sister and me in that same hallway in the middle of the night as we flew out of our bunk beds at a sharp crack of thunder. I hear him utter a cuss word for some reason as he washed his hands in the bathroom sink–and after seeing me standing there, wide-eyed, apologize. I recall Saturday mornings in the summer when I would go out and swing on the swing set, going so high the hollow metal legs would gently lift off the ground while Dad mowed the lawn. The smell of fresh-cut grass would waft up to me as I swung through the air; the birds chirped brightly in the morning sunshine.

On hot days we swam in the small, above-ground swimming pool in the backyard. I was too young to remember the baptism of my parents in that very pool, but I did witness other baptisms in the cool water.

People who had nowhere else to go lived in our basement at times, and in this house my mom and dad became foster parents to newborn babies awaiting adoption. Teenage cousins would stay for a week or so in the summer, and there were many trips back and forth to Detroit to visit our grandparents. Grandma Koelzer always kept a bag of marshmallows for us in the bottom drawer of her writing desk.

I also remember visiting the homes of people downtown and bringing bags of clothing and groceries. There was a small white plastic church on the kitchen table with a slit in the top to collect our loose change for the "Boat People" now fleeing war-torn Vietnam. Church consisted of weekly fellowship gatherings with like-minded believers at one house or another, evenings filled with guitar music and lots of kids. While I don't remember a family devotional time or memorizing Bible verses, worship was all around me.

Though I may be the only one of us kids to remember Frank and Lynda as baby believers, these glimmers of faith lived out in action spoke volumes to my ever-watching eyes. What I observed as a small girl is what I would later recognize as an immense gratitude for God's grace displayed in active love for each other, us kids, for neighbors and for strangers. It was as if Jesus was a verb to them.

Faith is simple for a child because it is often borrowed. I observed my parents' faith for a long time without recognizing it for what it was. I floated along in the whispery haven of my parents' love and home, absorbing without understanding the depth of their love and generosity toward others. I didn't question anything; I soaked it up and assumed all families were like mine.

Eventually I would learn that there was a Person behind their faith, a relationship that was not earthly but embodied in earthly relationships. I accepted that God was the Person, His son Jesus Christ that same person–fully God yet fully man. It would take many years for this to become even remotely understandable to me. But as a child I watched it and I believed in it, this something–Someone–so much bigger, so *Other*.

I didn't question the existence of this Person, for what I saw of Him was good.

◇ ◇ ◇

September 2005

The walls in my parents' freshly finished condo were a sunny yellow with red accents all around, true to my mother's gifted eye for style and color. The sunroom was already everyone's favorite place, a room filled with windows and green plants, soft, plump chairs, and a view of the community's central pond and visiting geese and ducks. "Sunshine on my shoulders makes me happy" is spelled out beneath one window–John Denver is a family favorite.

Jim and I and the kids walked in with a cooler in tow and baseball gloves in hand, ready to head to the park for another family gathering. Simeon and Victoria were visiting from Germany, and we planned to celebrate Sim's birthday. I hugged my brother and his girlfriend tight and admired the view from the sunroom windows. I took in the smell of new construction still in the air, seeing the green grass filling in below the window outside.

My dad the electrician had wired a million light switches with dimmers for every one of the lights in the place, and Mom and I cracked up because I could not for the life of me figure out which switch went to which light.

"Doesn't matter, Cher! The important thing is that it was done MY way!" Dad cackled and grinned as he rubbed his hands together.

At the park Dad was excited to show the kids a new kite he had bought–an outrageous fabrication of blues, reds, and yellows that looked as if it could fill the whole sky.

Jim helped him open the plastic wrap while the kids waited impatiently; together we unfolded the massive creation and untangled the lines. There was just a bit of wind, and it took several tries to heave the behemoth into the air. I watched as Dad became frustrated with the contraption, its weight and size proving to be too much for the limp breeze of the day.

"C'mon, Grandpa!" said Levi. "You can do it!"

"Grand-pa! Grand-pa!" Courtney chanted as she grinned and clapped her hands.

Jared managed the lines to keep them from becoming tangled again, but much to the kids' disappointment their grandpa gave up trying to launch the kite into the air. This struck me as odd; my father was usually persistent, especially when trying something new and exciting. Or when there was a problem to solve. But I pushed the thought away and refused to examine it up close.

Dad rolled up the kite and stuffed it into its packaging.

"Sorry kids, Grandpa's got a headache. We'll try again another day." The kids soon ran off to the swings and slide.

When we got back to the condo, he had stretched out on the couch with his eyes closed before the rest of us were entirely through the door.

Placing the kite and the leftovers from lunch on the table, Mom leaned near and murmured, "He hasn't been the same since he got back from Uncle Karl's funeral."

"Ah," I said. Now that would explain why he seemed "off," why he didn't seem like himself. Dad's older brother Karl lived in the Florida Keys and had recently passed away; Dad had just flown back home the day before. The trip and the emotion must have wiped him out.

But a couple of weeks later, Mom called me while we were in the middle of the kids' bath routine. Courtney wiggled in front of me as I attempted to comb through her wet hair while Audrey splashed in the tub. Jim and the boys were wrestling somewhere, loudly, while they waited for their turns for the (one) shower to be free.

I turned on Lawrence Welk on our tiny bedroom TV to keep Courtney distracted so I could pull through the snarls and concentrate on what Mom was telling me about Dad. After a nice dinner with their friends John and Diane, the guys decided to take the sailboat out on the water. At one point Dad attempted a jibe, to turn into the wind and catch it with the other side of the sail, but he became flustered and ran the boat aground on a sandbar.

She continued with quiet concern, relating another sailing incident when Dad and his friend Craig went out together. Dad had scraped the boat against a buoy in the channel, something careful sailors never do. The guys had privately shared with her their concern that something seemed a little off with their buddy Frankie. Mom confided to me that those two incidents scared Dad as well. At home, Mom was noticing that Dad seemed bored and tired and had little drive.

I clucked and "hmmmed" with Mom on the phone, still trying to comb through the knots in Courtney's thick hair. I was concerned but distracted enough to stuff down the flutter of worry that tap-tapped at my insides.

All business, I said, "Well, has he been to the doctor? We need more information."

"Yes, I've taken him a couple of times already. The medicine they've given him makes him dizzy; the headache won't go away. They think it's a sinus infection. But he's too dizzy to drive; I don't want him driving."

"But what about work?" I asked. Dad's commute from Zeeland to Esper Electric in Kalamazoo was now a 45-minute drive one way. He only had to make the drive for two more years. "Is he taking time off?"

"Well, yes, he's going to rest a few days and see if these meds will eventually help."

I held the phone with one hand and forcefully snapped my fingers at the boys with the other to get them to quiet down, but I heard Mom murmur on the phone, almost to herself, "He's not himself. Something's just not right."

It's hard to pinpoint the exact moment my parents became my friends, but one day in college remains vivid in my memory.

I sat in class with a blank index card on the desk in front of me. The professor had just asked us to write down the one thing that was the most important to us. I have no recollection of the point of this exercise or what she said afterward. Still, as I mentally filtered my priorities in life, I suddenly landed on the firm foundation that lived, breathed, and held me up: my family.

Though God was in there too–His presence was evident and indwelling inside of my family–He wasn't living inside of me yet. As I stripped away all the detritus of life–education, part-time job, dating, friends, and hobbies–I realized with sudden clarity that my parents were the one safe and solid unit that was constant in my life, the one place I could always return to no matter what condition I was in. They were my safety net.

I was 20 years old and, though diligently studying to become an elementary school teacher, my life was full of choices I was making that I knew my parents would not be proud of. Whether they were aware of them or not, there was no doubt in my mind of their love for me, of their support, and that they were on my team, always.

My parents loved me more than anyone else did. This realization was like a smooth road falling in place before my feet, a bridge over a rocky chasm. Upon this path I would continue forward in life, trusting that wherever the road took me, Mom and Dad would walk alongside me.

And I wanted them there.

After that epiphany, the thought of something happening to my parents, even an inkling of a scare, would paralyze me with sadness and fear. It is incredible how the mind can quickly take a notion, a hypothetical situation, and escalate it with little effort.

An unanswered phone call to them would prompt images of a car accident, or police showing up at my door in the middle of the night. When my thoughts wandered down this road, I would suddenly find myself with a lump in my throat and tears forming as I mentally prepared the eulogy for my parents' funeral. It was rash and overdramatic, but that's how a thought spiral works. It sucked me in time after time.

This time, though, was not hypothetical. This time there *was* something going on with Dad.

Later that night of the phone call with mom, after we bathed the kids and put them to bed, I lay awake next to Jim and pondered the conversation.

As a mother of four, I needed to discern on a regular basis what was a true emergency and what was exaggerated fear or drama. "He's breathing on me!" is not cause for genuine concern. Annoyance, yes; ambulance, no. "I'm bleeding!" can be, but not always.

Not that there have not been big things. When Courtney was born, the pediatrician heard a distinguishable heart murmur before she had been alive twenty-four hours. When more information showed that surgery would be necessary, I then allowed myself to cry.

I had learned to gather more information before reacting, both to conserve my energy and my emotions. As a form of self-protection, I prefer to use those sparingly. It's a significant investment to dig down deep and get all worked up, let alone cry.

I lay there trying to explain away my dad's symptoms, thinking maybe it was nothing.

After all, one of my parents' friends had a condition for a while where whenever she looked up, she became so dizzy she fainted; it eventually went away on its own.

And I knew I had read somewhere that an ear infection could cause a disturbance in the middle ear that could affect one's equilibrium. Maybe all Dad had was an ear infection.

As I fell asleep, I continued to search through snippets of random medical knowledge in my head and try to make sense of Dad's symptoms.

But I could not shake the image of my parents climbing aboard a roller-coaster ride and buckling in.

Days went by without much more insight into what was happening with Dad. While I drove my minivan full of kids to the grocery store, I tried to be honest with myself, which was another mental and emotional investment. The truth is, I just wanted it all to go away.

My life was busy. I was a stay-at-home mom whose days were full of "fooding," refereeing, laundry, Bible study, and bodily fluids. My most recent journal entry read, "Dear God, please don't let me die anytime soon, because apparently, I am the only one who knows how to change the toilet paper roll. Amen."

At Meijer, I grabbed a cart with a bench and buckled in Levi and Courtney. They immediately elbowed each other, Levi slapping his little stuffed animal against Courtney's arm.

Slap. "Ouch!"

Slap. "Levi!!"

Slap. "Mooom!!"

I slipped Audrey into the seat of another cart, clicked the strap around her belly, then handed her off to Jared. He dutifully pushed his cart behind me through the aisles, hamming it up to make his sister giggle.

I was concerned for my parents but told myself that the Lord would take care of them, that Dad would start to feel better eventually. I willed myself to believe that this, too, shall pass. I just … I didn't need to worry unless we had a real reason to. Right?

I absentmindedly checked off my grocery list and put back the Cocoa Crispies and Oreos the kids kept sneaking into the carts, thinking I didn't see them.

I refused to believe that something serious could be wrong with Dad. They had just moved to their new condo, their nest was officially empty, and Dad was almost retired. They were so happy to be looking forward. How could God allow it? Why would he?

I heaved the loaded grocery cart and precious cargo into the checkout lane with superhuman strength. Behind me, Jared's cart ran into my heels. Again.

And, on top of that, I argued in my head, *don't I have enough to deal with right now? Four busy kids, a husband who travels a lot for work, church ministries I'm involved in, a daughter with special needs. Would you really add something serious to our lives right now, God?*

Sliding back into the driver's seat of the van, the kids all buckled up and the groceries haphazardly loaded, I bowed my head over the steering wheel as I recognized the real root of my questions.

Please, God, don't let it be serious.

Don't sever my safety net.

CHAPTER 3

All the days ordained for me
were written in your book before one of them came to be.

Psalm 139:16 NIV

October 2005

To the Team at Esper Electric,

First: the medical facts. I have some growth spots on my brain. What's a couple of extra golf balls to a guy who doesn't golf? We do not have a definitive diagnosis, so there is no prognosis. Are we concerned? You bet. Are we scared? Absolutely. It doesn't look great.

Are we hopeless? NO WAY. There is a God, and He knows my name.

Do I pray for healing? Yes! But I have been more than healed, and I am so thankful that God has given me what I have had.

Good thing you can't see the tears on my keyboard.

Here is how I explain this to my friends:

I have so many people who love me, what else can you want?

I have been blessed with a loving, understanding wife, and we raised a BUNCH of really great kids. And we already have eight grandkids, who are so special. To touch and be touched by such people is the greatest treasure on earth.

If that isn't enough, I "married" your son-in-law Mike in 1985. When we went to sign the incorporation papers, that was exactly what I told him. And he has been a friend, an upstanding business partner, and a great guy.

WAIT. I've got more. I have this successful company with so many people I cherish and respect. Do you know that they even have a saying, "Do it the Esper Way," and what that means is "to do it right"? And my last name is Esper! WOW.

I am not a quitter. I am a troubleshooter, as most of these guys know. I am going to work with my doctors to find out what this is and how to get it under control.

Another thing I am is a planner, so as my daughter Miriam keeps saying, "Dad, you have put together such a great transition team."

All of us are in God's care. And I am not worried for any of you or your families. You will all do well.

This is not goodbye, just a "catch you later." I love you all. And thanks Mike for being such a good guy. You and Scott will do fine.

I have achieved 70 years' worth of fulfillment in a mere 61 years.

Frank

Team Esper Captain

Today I am waiting for the results from Dad's MRI. Are the spots in his brain cancer or not? In my fretting, I need to DO something to create a sense of control that will fill the pit in my stomach. The grass is thick in the yard, so I decide to go out and mow, telling myself that I'll do it so Jim doesn't have to when he comes home from his business trip.

Mowing is soothing. I was taught behind a push mower on our acre of yard in Otsego. Reneé and I often shared the job, each taking a turn doing a strip across and back, resting while the other took her turn. It was not a chore we enjoyed, but Dad paid us to do it and, as an adult, I have a new appreciation for the task. Not only is it productive, but it turns chaos into order; it's an accomplishment that you can look upon fondly for a few days before it needs to be done again.

Our yard in Schoolcraft is small, the backyard more challenging because of the swing set, the sandbox, the pool, the patio, and the shed. Lots of obstacles. But the front yard is relatively easy, with just a couple of trees that disrupt the steady, soothing back and forth.

After making sure the kids are ensconced safely in front of the TV in the basement, I put in my earbuds and find a good sermon on my iPod to listen to. My desire for control is humming loudly inside of me today; creating rows of crisp cut grass and taking in some pragmatic teaching of the Word is just what I need.

I start up the mower, cut a nice fresh row or two along the curb, then notice that Jared is waving me down from the front porch. At 10, he is my eyes-on-the-ground reporter when I am not in the house.

I shut off the mower and pull out an earbud.

"Courtney won't stop singing; we can't hear the TV!" he reports.

"Okay, send her out here," I say, starting the mower again to squeeze in a couple more rows.

Courtney follows Jared out the front door a minute later, her hands over her ears until I turn off the mower. I tell her that she can sing all she wants, but she'll have to go somewhere else so that the others can hear the TV.

"But Mom..." she says dramatically, hands outstretched. "I HAVE to SING!"

"But we can't HEAR!" Jared argues.

"Court, how 'bout you go swing on the swing set so you can sing as loud as you want, and you won't bother the others."

"Okay, Mom!" Happily, she runs around to the backyard where she can swing and sing to her heart's content. Jared watches with his hands on his hips and then heads back inside.

I start up the mower again, leaving one earbud out because I know there will be more interruptions.

Sure enough, I get about three more rows done before I see that Audrey is on the porch now, holding out her sippy cup.

I turn off the mower.

"What's the matter, honey?"

"I want more juice." She sticks out her belly and squints her eyes at me.

"Try that again." I say, the correction automatic. "How do you ask?"

"Please, can I have ... more juice?" Now she sticks her butt out and makes a face. She's the cutest thing in the world, this blonde tornado.

"Yes. But ask Jared if he will pour some for you, okay? Mommy's going to finish mowing."

As Audrey bunny hops back through the front door, I start the mower again.

Pretty soon, Levi comes bounding out through the garage, a yellow plastic bat and whiffle ball in his hand. I figured he'd get bored with the TV quickly.

He stands on the driveway, hollering, "Mom, mom! Mom! Mom!" I see his mouth moving, but I can't hear his voice.

I turn off the mower.

"Watch this!" He throws the plastic ball into the air and quickly swings the bat, missing the ball by a mile.

"Oh, good try, buddy!" I smile, giving him a thumbs up.

He scrambles after the ball and tries again. And again. And again.

"Mom, watch!"

"Mom, watch!"

"Mom, watch!"

"I'm going to finish mowing now, bud, okay? Keep trying!"

"Wait, wait, Mom! One more time!" He's swinging with everything he's got.

I give him another thumbs up and start the mower again.

In my mind, I picture my neighbors hearing the mower start, then stop, then start, then stop, shaking their heads and thinking, "Cheryl must be mowing again ..."

Then Jared comes out again to the front porch, this time with the cordless phone in his hand.

"Mom, it's Aunt Reneé!" he calls when I turn off the mower yet again.

It's the call I've been waiting for. My heart drops, and everything in me clenches tight. *Dear God, let this be some good news.*

I take the phone from Jared.

"It's cancer," Reneé says, brokenly.

My body goes limp now, emptying all breath. *Oh, Dad.*

Reneé's two words have answered my immediate question but left a dozen more in their wake. She sniffles as she gives me more appointment times and tests to come; we are not on the phone long. I take the phone up to my bedroom and, with tears, I call Jim, who is in San Diego for work. I explain that the three tumors found a month ago in my father's brain are indeed cancerous.

My dad's voice on the phone days later, thin with exhaustion, tells me the news is only getting worse. Though they still don't know the primary source of the cancer, the prognosis is not good: his life expectancy is six months to a year with treatment, three to four months without. The brain tumors are inoperable. His voice trembles.

I reach into the well of my faith and offer him cupped hands of hope in platitudes. "God is in control. We will take one day at a time. Nothing is impossible with God." Words

I believe with all my being to be true, but at this moment cannot reach through the phone line and heal my father. Words that ring hollow and fall to the floor as tears, leaving wet marks on my shoes.

Numbly, Jim and I put the kids to bed that night. Afterward I come downstairs and pull on a sweatshirt. I head out the door, into the dark, to walk the neighborhood and wrestle with God.

As I look up into the deep autumn sky, I breathe deeply, my face flushed with agony. Jim and I have been married thirteen years, and though our life is full of small comforts and sweet children, a contented but regular life, it has not lacked pain. But tonight, my faith is a rope stretched taut, fibers popping and tearing.

While the stars sparkle above me and tears pour down my face, I clench my fists and declare to God, "Well, you might as well rip my heart out of my chest and crush it between your fingers!"

I sob as I walk, not caring if the neighbors hear or see. I run out of Kleenex and wipe my nose on my sleeve. My grief is hostile.

Ultimatums run through my head and spew from my mouth in an angry prayer.

"You'd better heal him, Lord!"

And then, chastened in spite of myself, I whimper. "I know you are able, but will you? Will you? How could you do this to Mom? What about her? I know Dad loves you, I know he's headed for heaven... but now, Lord? Why *now*?"

I go on like this for a while, pleading desperately, bawling.

Suddenly, different questions enter my thoughts. Is God questioning *me*?

Do you trust me? Will you still believe if he is not healed?

Haven't I answered this question with my life already? Haven't we already walked this road of "healing" with Courtney? Though we had prayed for a miracle, her heart surgery had been corrected by surgeons, her diagnosis now encompassed by therapists and educators. After those first five years I had finally stopped crying.

But this is not Courtney; it's my dad. My *dad.* Though both are my flesh and blood, one is my offspring, the other my origin. My foundation is crumbling, the ground shifting beneath my feet.

And there are more questions.

If my dad does die, is God still good?

Is He still God?

I was nine years old again, and it was a windy day in early spring.

The lot to the east of our new house in Otsego was a large empty field; my dad mowed paths through it from our yard to the neighbors on the other side. An immense farm field lay behind us to the north, stretching to the tree-lined horizon. And on the northeast corner of our large backyard was a single wooden fence post that marked the spot where the three properties converged.

The post came to my chest, but somehow I managed to pull myself up to sit on the top of it. Balancing myself precariously, I took in the beautiful, raw landscape. In the middle of the farm field stood an enormous grandfather of an oak tree. I gazed admiringly upon that tree; it seemed so solid as it stood out there, alone and majestic.

I didn't know what made me think about God at that moment; maybe it was the tree. Perhaps it was because I felt so singularly small atop that lone post, an island in an ocean of tall grass and wildflowers, plowed dirt and freshly cut grass. The sky seemed enormous; the tree line so distant.

As I thought about God, my nine-year-old self decided I needed to assess his abilities right then and there. I asked him to do a miracle and lift me in the air, right off that post. Just for a minute, not too high. Just to show me he could do it ... if he *could* do it.

I closed my eyes, folding my hands together beneath my chin. I was a perfect picture of subservience.

I was silent, but urged in my head, "C'mon God ..."

I imagined my mother glancing up from her sewing machine through the upstairs window, stunned, witness to a miracle, her oldest daughter suspended in mid-air.

Nothing happened.

The wind lifted my plain brown hair. I released a finger from my posture of prayer and pushed my glasses up on my nose.

But my bottom stayed put on top of that post.

I didn't want God to feel bad or think I was disappointed in Him. I was probably a little weird for asking, I rationalized. Who was I to request such a thing? I was just a shy, bookish fourth grader. I looked up at the sky thoughtfully, then shrugged my shoulders.

"Okay, then." I hopped down off the post.

Many years later, I wonder why that didn't bother me at the time. Why I didn't throw my hands up in the air with a sarcastic retort: "Wow, way to go, God. You're so powerful." Or "Well, I guess you're a fake."

I didn't go running to my parents to tell on God. I didn't angrily accuse them of making him up.

I only remember having a solid certainty in my heart that if he had wanted to, he could have done it. With child-like faith I accepted that he didn't want to, today.

I realize now that God gave me a gift that day. A gift of faith that would grow, would falter, and would grow some more. He had planted tiny seeds in my heart that day of acceptance ... surrender ... trust.

And so tonight, this starry, sad October night, I cannot answer these questions running through my head with anything but *yes*.

But surrendering to the very real possibility that Dad may die feels like betrayal, and it rips through my heart and soul.

Which requires more faith? To believe that God can lift me off a fence post and suspend me in mid-air? Or to believe that He is still God when he chooses not to?

◇ ◇ ◇

1980

My family had moved to Otsego in 1978; nine months later, my sister Miriam was born. By the time she was a year old, I was ten, and Dad had camping fever.

One warm Saturday morning, after riding along with Dad on his regular jaunt to Bob's Hardware, I hopped out of the van and followed him into a new store called Outdoor World. I was immediately drawn to an inviting display in the center of the store: a huge tent set up with cozy sleeping bags laid out inside. An open cooler sat nearby filled with cans of pop and snacks.

I sat in one of the camp chairs by the fake campfire while Dad talked with the guy behind the counter, taking in all the cool camping gear available in the store. There were tents, sleeping bags, and hammocks in all sizes, colorful hanging lights to decorate the campsite, and pans of popcorn ready to be popped over an open fire. To a kid who preferred to be indoors with a book most times, this definitely made the outdoors look fun!

I heard Dad say in awe, "Isn't that slick!" and then call to me. "Cheri, come over here and look at this!" I walked over to where the salesman was setting up some metal cots, one on top of the other, like bunk beds.

"You and Reneé could sleep on these, and we'll get some nice warm sleeping bags for all you kids. What do you think?" His grin was contagious; I could practically see the travel plans formulating in his head.

Dad had taken us on a few camping trips the last couple of summers, borrowing a tent or a small pull-behind camper. The summer before last Mom had been pregnant, and camping was just not fun with morning sickness. Last summer, Miriam was too small to take camping. One night we had to settle for "camping" by sleeping out in the van in the backyard.

But now Dad was getting serious. And I was right there with him.

"Those are so cool, Dad! Can I have a red sleeping bag?" I asked, running my hands along the soft flannel lining.

When we finally left the store, Dad had purchased a tent that could sleep ten, the bunking cots, sleeping bags for all, an air mattress for him and mom, a Coleman stove, and a powerful lantern.

His enthusiasm for technology bubbled over as he described to me on the drive home how sophisticated this new tent was.

"No more heavy, wet canvas, Cher, like my old pup tent! This new stuff they use is strong but lightweight, so we won't get too hot. Best of all, it'll keep us nice and dry!"

For the first trip with the new gear, Dad decided to take us camping with Uncle Barney and Aunt Jo, his oldest brother and his wife. They owned a motorhome and camped all the time; now that their four children were older, they often camped kid-free.

"They're here! They're here!" I yelled with excitement as Uncle Barney and Aunt Jo backed their massive camper into the site next to ours. I couldn't wait to go inside their motorhome, a miniature house on wheels. I had been in it a handful of times when they would visit and "camp" in our driveway. The tiny kitchen, the big bed above the driver's seat, even their own bathroom was all so cozy.

While I eagerly explored their camper, Uncle Barney pulled out an extension cord and plugged it in, and they were set up. Within minutes of arriving, they were sitting at their picnic table smoking cigarettes.

"Cheri!" Dad hollered out to me. "Come help us set up the tent!"

I held up poles while Dad drove stakes into the ground, then watched over Miriam while Mom hefted her playpen inside the tent. Dad toyed with the propane stove, unfolded our cots, and inflated the air mattress. Reneé set up the camp chairs and Simeon laid out sleeping bags.

Finally, Dad and Mom joined Barney and Jo at their picnic table, sweaty and tired. Pretty soon they were talking politics–the Reagan/Carter election was that fall–and I took Miriam from my mom's arms.

"Can we take her and go to the playground, Mom?" I asked.

"Alright, just keep a close eye on your brother, too."

Reneé and I spun our brother on the merry-go-round until he turned green, then ran back and forth from the swings to the slide. As I kept Miriam busy in the sandbox, it began to sprinkle. I put her back in her stroller, and we all headed back to our campsite; the gentle rain sounded soothing under Uncle Barney's awning.

But the wind soon picked up, and that gentle patter turned into a heavy, drenching rain. While my aunt and uncle walked up the three steps into their camper and closed the door, my family huddled on the ground inside our tent.

As Dad zipped up the tent windows, I saw Uncle Barney's hand reach out from the motorhome; with a flick of the wrist his awning rolled up like a magic carpet. The awning at the front of our tent flapped and fought like a trapped kite desperate to soar.

After a few minutes of heavy rain, I noticed that the corners of the tent roof were beginning to fill up with rainwater, and I hoped desperately that this tent was as strong as Dad said it was.

There was a flash of lightning and a loud clap of thunder, and the younger kids began to cry. My focus was on the roof of the tent, now sagging under the weight of those pockets of water. Mom's eyes kept flickering up there too, as Dad repeated, "Don't worry, kids! This tent is not going to let us get wet!"

True, we were still dry. Though Dad tried to convey confidence in this high-tech nylon and metal structure, I found myself wondering, *at what point do we make a run for Uncle Barney's motorhome?*

Finally, Dad stood up and began to gently press against the bulging sacs of water at the corners, pushing them up and over to dump the water onto the ground outside. Mom joined him, but the rain was pooling in the corners of the tent as fast as they were emptied.

My little gut clamped down on the fear bubbling there as I watched my parents' efforts, Mom struggling to hold Miriam and push on the tent roof with one hand. I clenched my hands in my lap and felt a lump in my throat. My heart hammered in my chest along with the thunder, and I jiggled my crossed legs nervously. I was trying hard not to envision the tent collapsing, my family trapped in a heap of muddy sleeping bags.

I'm too big to cry, I thought to myself. *I am almost 11. I'm starting middle school in the fall; is this how a middle-schooler would act?*

Silently, I stood up on tiptoe and began to push against the water pockets to help get the water off the roof and onto the ground. As the rain fell and the wind blew, the tears wanted to come but I choked them back. *I will not cry.*

The rain finally began to let up, and Mom suddenly noticed my face. I was sniffling–not crying–but my fear had been discovered.

"Cheri, honey, are you scared?" she asked. "We're okay, we're okay," she said, shifting Miriam to her other hip and putting her arm around me. In her embrace the floodgates opened, and I sobbed uncontrollably.

I choked out the words, "But I'm not supposed to cry! I CAN'T cry! I'm the oldest!"

Through my tears I noticed my parents exchanging a look of surprise at this self-inflicted burden.

Though Dad attempted to add adventure and spontaneity to my family's life, somewhere on the road between nine and ten I had placed upon my shoulders the weight of my own expectations–to be good, to be strong, to be responsible.

On a hot day in the summer of 1983, though Dad was on break from teaching at Kalamazoo Valley Community College, he and his lab assistant Mike were hard at work. Together they had taken on electrical jobs at new construction sites to glean experience that would help them help their students.

As they finished the electrical service on a new build, they sat still for a few minutes under the sun on the roof.

"Well, Mike, what do you think?" Dad asked as he took a drink of water. "Do you think we could do this for a living?" The two had been toying with the idea of starting up their own electric company for a while now, to take what they had been teaching and turn it into a business.

"Yeah," replied Mike. "I really think we could. I can just see it," he said as he waved his hand over the neighborhood, over Dad's Vega station wagon and his own Chevy pickup. "In ten years, I bet we could have ten company trucks on the road and ten electricians of our own."

"Well then, let's do it!" Dad grinned confidently. A year later, Dad had my brother Simeon design a logo–a superhero-like lightning bolt they dubbed "E-Man" – and Esper Electric was born.

Dad's understanding of electrical theory and his math and engineering skills, combined with Mike's construction expertise, allowed them to form a well-organized residential and commercial electrical company. They drew from the pool of students that passed through KVCC's Industrial Electricity program to find hardworking, capable employees.

Through years of hard work, hard truths, and hard games of racquetball, Dad and Mike forged a partnership centered on trust, integrity, and faith in Christ. As Dad joked to Mike on the day they signed the papers, "It's like a marriage...but without the sex!"

2005

By 2005 the company was twenty-one years old and going strong, with twenty-two trucks and forty employees. Mike's "rooftop vision" had inspired Dad, who was always ready to rise to a challenge.

Today Mike is sitting across from Dad at the new white dining table in the condo. Craig is there too; not only is he a long-time friend of both men, but he is also the insurance agent who oversees the coverage of all things Esper Electric.

It's a sunny fall day, and Mom carries over glasses of iced beverages for everyone from the kitchen as they begin this painful task of discussing the future of the business. Reneé is in town and I am visiting for the day; we sit on Mom's red couches talking quietly and pretending not to listen, pretending not to comprehend the weight of this meeting.

Craig clears his throat and begins by reading a passage of Scripture that he has chosen especially for this moment, from the book of 1 Peter, chapter 1.

"Blessed be the God and Father of our Lord Jesus Christ, who according to His great mercy has caused us to be born again to a living hope through the resurrection of Jesus Christ from the dead, to obtain an inheritance which is imperishable and undefiled and will not fade away, reserved in heaven for you, who are protected by the power of God through faith for a salvation ready to be revealed in the last time.

"In this you greatly rejoice, even though now for a little while if necessary, you have been distressed by various trials, so that the proof of your faith, being more precious than gold which is perishable, even though tested by fire, may be found to result in praise and glory and honor at the revelation of Jesus Christ; and though you have not seen Him, you love Him, and though you do not see Him now, but believe in Him, you greatly rejoice with joy inexpressible and full of glory, obtaining as the outcome of your faith the salvation of your souls."

(1 Peter 1:3-9 NASB)

He continues with verse 13: *"Therefore, prepare your minds for action, keep sober in spirit, fix your hope completely on the grace to be brought to you at the revelation of Jesus Christ."*

I marvel at the gift given to Dad of such a strong circle of believers around him, as his business partner, as his insurance guy. And not that they are just fellow believers, but they are true friends.

As Dad looks his forced retirement square in the face, the three men begin the painful process of severing Dad's part in the ownership of the business. This event will ensure that Mom is well taken care of, and that there will be no loose ends for her to deal with if this cancer does end Dad's life. For that I am grateful.

And though I can feel my gut tightening at the thought of what all these signatures imply, I ponder the Scriptures that Craig chose to read today.

I understand that Peter's letter was written to encourage Christians who were being persecuted in Rome, but it is very fitting for today. Dad is going through a persecution of his own, not for being a Christian, but a trial that will test his faith to the very depths of his core.

If Dad meets Jesus early because of this cancer or is miraculously healed and lives another thirty years, I am humbled by the very promise of this lovely, pure, and indestructible inheritance that waits for him. Only God can reveal when Dad will receive it.

Chapter 4

Come ye that love the Lord, and let your joys be known,
Join in a song with sweet accord,
join in a song with sweet accord,
And thus surround the throne,
and thus surround the throne.
We're marching to Zion, beautiful, beautiful Zion,
We're marching upward to Zion, the beautiful city of God.

"Marching to Zion" by Isaac Watts
(Public Domain)

November 8, 2005

Good morning, friends and saints,

Ever had to talk with a fat tongue? Well, typing now is like typing with a fat finger. Even though I read what I type, I am glad Miriam will be the real spell-checker.

It is just 1:00 a.m. on Tuesday; we get to talk with a nurse and doctor in just 36 hours at the Cancer Treatment

Center of America in Zion, IL. They have five days of testing and intake scheduled for Wed, Thursday, Fri, Mon, and Tuesday. We do not know when or if treatments will start until we meet. But we are so glad to get on the road tomorrow. Lynda has the keys, so we will gas-up, mocha-up, get a paper, and she will transport us.

We have reservations at a resort they recommend, nice and close to their hospital. They said we will be together for the beginning, meaning I won't be hospitalized immediately. The waiting is harder than I would have thought; I guess I am pretty used to charging ahead.

I feel fine on the outside and have no pain inside, other than emotional fatigue. I have an appetite but am slowly losing a little weight.

I hope you have visited frankesper.com, so nicely put together by my nephew Mike with help from Miriam. All the prayers, emails, and many cards via mail have encouraged me to know so many wonderful people in my full life. The Scriptures you send are all read carefully.

My favorite saying we found this summer in Maine on our trip with John and Diane was, "The winds of grace are always blowing. It is up to you to raise your sails."

So tomorrow we will hoist sail and set off in a W-S-W tack and veer due north after we round the bottom of the lake. Should have an ETA of 4:00 p.m. so we can scout the land and make a safe harbor for the night before our meeting on Wednesday.

Don't expect to know a whole lot more for a week after that except perhaps to get a scalp job and start some treatments.

God Bless you all for your love and support. Jesus Reigns. Frank

As Miriam flew past a toll booth on the I-80/90 toll road toward Chicago, I cursed my horrific map-reading skills. I was trying to trace our route to Zion, Illinois, on a crumpled map when she cried out, "Oh no! Did I just miss the toll?" She briefly took her foot off the gas.

I looked up from the map.

"Uhhh...yep. You did. Don't worry about it, they probably got a picture of your license plate and will send you a bill."

I uttered a half-laugh as I returned to the map. I was too distracted and worried to think about this minor detail. Obviously Miriam was too, as she put the pedal to the metal again.

I was in the passenger seat of Miriam's minivan, her baby son Elijah buckled into the back seat, and we were headed to the Cancer Treatment Center after receiving an urgent phone call from Mom earlier this evening.

She and Dad had finally made the much-anticipated trip a couple of days before and settled into a nearby hotel before they checked in to the Center. Dad immediately started radiation therapy on his head and began the prep for a colonoscopy the following day.

They had approached this visit to the CTCA with such hope, looking and praying for answers and treatment plans. Up to this point steroids had been keeping Dad's headaches at bay, but on check-in day he was unusually bloated and miserable, even running a fever. Despite his optimism and cheery hopes, the ride over was physically difficult. When he arrived for his colonoscopy appointment at the Center he could hardly move, so the doctor immediately ordered a CT scan that revealed a perforated bowel and a gut filled with infection. They scheduled surgery for 8 p.m.

My mom was not one to become frantic. She was not a yeller; she had always been good at remaining calm in an intense situation. So, when I heard her say on the phone earlier, "You might want to come over here tonight," though her voice was calm I knew something was up. After she explained what was going on, I quickly called Miriam, who lived an hour north of me, and we made plans for her to pick me up on the way to Illinois. Neither of us liked the idea of Mom sitting all alone while Dad was in surgery, 200 miles away from home.

I found myself pressing my own foot to the floor as if to make the van move even faster. Construction caused traffic to slow, and I wanted to stick my head out the window and scream, "I need to get to my parents!" I was amazed that the river of vehicles hadn't parted before us to let us through. Didn't they know?

The cell phone in my hand vibrated with a loud buzz when a call came in. It was my mom again, and this time I could hear a thread of panic in her voice.

"Where are you?"

"We've got about an hour left. How's Dad?"

"He's in surgery now." She hesitated. "I – I just think I should tell you that the doctor said there is a chance he may not survive this operation."

I swallowed hard and closed my eyes. *Lord in heaven. Please. Please.*

"Okay. We'll be there soon. We're praying. Don't stop praying, Mom!" I felt desperation creeping into my voice.

I relayed the message to Miriam, who cried out and clutched the rosary that had been in her palm since we left. After she called her husband Seth, asking him to pray without ceasing, I called Jim, then Reneé, and asked them to do the same.

I looked out the window into the dark that flew by, an abyss of unknown painted in the sky. A defiant anger rose up in my chest.

"No," I thought as my fists clenched in my lap. "This is not how this is going to end. It can't be." Though I felt like I was demanding something from God, I also had a deep knowing in my gut that He could handle it.

But He didn't owe me anything, and that terrified me.

I closed my eyes and prayed.

Many years later, reflecting on that night, Mom told us that while Miriam and I drove furiously north, she fidgeted in the waiting room, then wandered the hallway. After a while she decided to walk up to the lobby near the main entrance of the hospital, hoping to greet us there when we arrived.

The lobby of the Cancer Center was gorgeous and welcoming, with glass walls and towering green plants. Soft lamplight and fresh flowers in vases graced the information desk and every side table. One wall was covered with rough-hewn slabs carved with the names of cancer survivors. On a nearby plaque the term "survivor" was defined as someone who has been in remission for five years or more. She carefully read each name, laying her palm on the bricks as if to draw strength and hope from them. Closing her eyes and taking a deep breath, she was immediately filled with what can only be described as a peace that passes all understanding.

Mom would tell me with a gentle smile and a tilt of her head that though she was not given a picture of the future, she clearly sensed the presence of the One who would remain with her no matter what the future held, and she was comforted.

Miriam and I finally arrived and were directed downstairs to a basement hallway where the operating and waiting rooms were. Pushing Elijah in the stroller, we saw Mom walking the hallway, alone, at the same time she looked up and saw us. We fell into each other's arms and she said, "It's okay, it's okay. The doctor has said that everything went well. Dad will be moved to recovery soon."

"You want to hear something funny?" she chuckled. "After Dad prayed with the surgeon and they were preparing to wheel him into the OR, I leaned close and whispered,

'It's okay, Frankie. I've got the joy, joy, joy, joy, down in my heart.' And he said, with his eyes closed and a grin on his face, 'Where?'"

We all laughed, and anvils of worry slid off our shoulders onto the cold tile floor. Dad would be okay.

Miriam pulled little Elijah from the stroller, a cherubic source of light and hope in the dark basement hallway. We cuddled him and passed him around, buoyant with the news that we would see Dad soon in recovery.

In my heart I fervently gave thanks to God, as well as a sheepish apology for my demanding prayers of earlier. I knew that this answered prayer had nothing to do with me, and everything to do with a gracious and merciful God.

Wearing a robe over his hospital gown and holding shakily onto the walker in front of him, I.V. pole trailing behind, Dad turned to me slowly. "Cher, did your mom just go…whissp?.." His eyes were round and his pointer finger bobbed up to the ceiling. We were slowly making our way down the hallway to get Dad out of his room and moving a bit. Trying to make light of his hallucination, I gently told him that no, Mom didn't just disappear into the ceiling in front of him. She was getting a cup of coffee and would meet us back in his room in a few minutes.

"I swear she was just standing in front of me," he muttered as we slowly kept walking. Prayers for my dad that had not stopped since I left my house three days before continued to roll through my head, and after a few more steps my dad began to whistle, always a good sign. "*This is my story, this is my song; praising my Savior, all the day long....*"

It had been a rough few days since the surgery. Dad's bowel had been repaired, God's mercy saving his life in that moment; but he now sported a fun, fragrant little bag that hung on the outside of his stomach. While he was upbeat and talkative right after surgery, his mood increased to an almost maniacal high as the day progressed. The doctor making rounds referred to him kindly as a "loquacious historian." This would have been funny if I hadn't been so terrified.

Either he was suffering side effects from the anesthesia or the tumors in his brain had been stimulated, turning him into a crazy man. For two frightening days my dad was someone I could not recognize and did not know what to do with, as he talked incessantly without making sense to people he thought he was seeing. He tried several times to pull the oxygen tube out of his nose, and at one point threw his arms dramatically across the bed and shouted, "Father! Into your hands I commit my spirit!"

Though I felt helpless, during it all my mom remained calm and soothing, holding his hand, talking gently to him. I often found her singing every hymn and Jesus song she knew, while practically laying on top of him, forcing him to look in her eyes, singing into his face:

"Precious Lord, take my hand,
Lead me on, help me stand;
I am tired, I am weak, I am worn..."

Finally, his mind calmed down and he began to return to himself.

We will never know for sure whether the bowel perforation was related to the cancer or the steroids in Dad's body, or if it was a separate issue. But it was a large hurdle to overcome before the cancer could be addressed once more.

After a two-week stay at the CTCA in Zion, with surgery and several radiation treatments behind him, Dad and Mom buckled back into their minivan–and their rollercoaster–and headed home for Thanksgiving.

CHAPTER 5

Before the mountains were brought forth,
or ever you had formed the earth and the world,
from everlasting to everlasting you are God.

Psalm 90:2 ESV

1980

"Cheri, do you want to send a note to Uncle Harry and Aunt Diane?" asked my dad. He handed me his finished letter and pointed to space at the bottom.

"Yeah!" I eagerly reached for the paper and added my own words in loopy cursive:

I'm so excited to see you! We have a new tent and we got bunked cots for me and Reneé! I can't wait to see the mountains! Dad says we should be there by the end of July, Lord willing! (Whatever that means!)

I signed my name with a heart over the i and handed it back to Dad, who chuckled as he read my ten-year-old enthusiasm and innocent Christianese. He tucked the letter into an envelope, sealed it, and placed a stamp in the corner. It would arrive at its destination in Boulder, Colorado, by the end of the week; and in two more months, so would we.

Dad was now planning a massive, three-week camping excursion all the way from Michigan to Colorado and back. Miriam was about a year and half old now, we were in between foster babies, and Mom was especially excited to go because it was her oldest sister we would be visiting in the mountains.

The relationship between my parents and Mom's sister Diane, 18 years her senior, and her husband Harry was special–they had been key influences in drawing my parents closer to Christ and into the Bible.

After several conversations with a recently born-again nephew, Uncle Harry, a WWII veteran and staunch atheist, vowed to read through the entire Bible just so he could disprove it. Though I don't know the details of his journey, I know that this resulted in him becoming an ardent and faithful follower of Jesus, as did his wife. They went on to lead fellowship meetings in their home and live out their faith before the eyes of their ten children, as well as a plethora of grandchildren, for the rest of their lives.

Uncle Harry and Aunt Di had moved from Detroit to Boulder, Colorado, around 1979, stopping by our house just north of Kalamazoo on their way out of the state. The seeds were soon planted for a Big Visit to the Rocky Mountains.

For the trip, my dad purchased an enclosed wooden trailer to carry all our camping equipment, which he painted brown to match our full-size van. Except that our van was green. Did I mention Dad was colorblind?

Mom planned meals, filled a cooler, and turned an old black steamer trunk into a pantry of sorts by stapling thick bands of elastic inside the lid to hold paper plates, napkins, paper towel, and plasticware, along with our dry goods. It all was loaded into the brown trailer with the tent, our cots, camp chairs, firewood, the Coleman stove, an enormous lantern, and our sleeping bags. We were ready to go.

Always one to keep up with the latest technology, Dad installed an 8-track cassette player under the steering wheel and loaded up the dash with a stack of John Denver tapes. I had "Rocky Mountain High" memorized by the time we got to the Indiana border.

Reneé and I raced each other back to the campsite from the pool, followed by Dad and Sim, to find Miriam sitting in a large bucket filled with warm soapy water.

"I take a baf!" she told us proudly, splashing at the bubbles and grinning through her chubby cheeks. Holding her baby doll up to Mom, who was soaping her up with a washcloth, she demanded, "Wash Baby Seben, too!"

Later, as Baby Seven hung on the makeshift clothesline to dry, we recounted our adventures at the pool to Mom over dinner at the picnic table. Between bites of crunchy tacos, I told her, "Dad let me stand on his shoulders while he walked down the slope to the deep end! It looked just like I was STANDING in the deep end of the pool!" Turning to

Dad I said with admiration, "How do you hold your breath that long?" Dad grinned and leaned into me, saying, "I'm just full of a lot of hot air!"

Reneé boasted that she could do three underwater somersaults in a row now, and Simeon had discovered that if he plugged his nose and went underwater, he could lift up his feet and float.

"He'll be swimming any day now!" Dad said proudly.

At the campfire that night, my eyes were heavy with sleep as I sat in my camp chair and tried to do a word search by the light of the fire. Snuggled into my sleeping bag on my cot for the night (my turn for the top bunk!), I fell asleep, waterlogged, exhausted, and smiling.

We established a loose routine for each day of travel: In the morning Dad would take down the emptied tent, fold it up into a long rectangle, and let Reneé and I roll back and forth on it to remove any trapped air so that it could be stuffed into its storage bag. This was our favorite job.

Once we were loaded into the car, Dad would drive us up to the bathroom building, and Mom would hand him a towel and his toothbrush. He'd take a 2-minute shower while we waited and then hop back into the driver's seat, whistling "On the Road Again."

In the car I would sing along with John Denver, his folksy guitar serenading me through the sweeping countryside. We sang songs about country roads, Muhlenberg County, and Grandma's feather bed. I thanked God I was a country boy (girl) and I, too, believed I was Mother Nature's Son–well, daughter.

Each day consisted of about six to eight hours of driving before arriving at the next KOA campground to set up the tent and beds. We would then swim in the pool or lake offered by the campground, eat dinner, and fall into our sleeping bags.

Dad planned our trip to take us from southwest Michigan, through Indiana, Illinois, Wisconsin, and Minnesota. We stayed a little longer in South Dakota, where we stopped to see the famous Corn Palace, Wall Drug, and Mount Rushmore. At one campground we participated in a Chuck Wagon dinner. We ate like cowboys–baked beans on tin plates–and went horseback riding after dinner.

Reneé and I had set up our "kingdom" in the very back of the van. We laid a blanket on the floor and played endless games of gin rummy while snacking on Starburst candies. We diligently recorded in our activity books all the states represented by the license plates of the cars we passed. And then one day, after driving through the southeast corner of Wyoming, we finally crossed the state line into Colorado. In the distance were the majestic Rocky Mountains and–appearing as if just to welcome us–a rainbow above them.

We devoted an entire week to our visit with Uncle Harry and Aunt Di in Boulder. We were thrilled when they drove us by the house pictured in the opening credits of our favorite TV show, "Mork and Mindy." They led us through the festive atmosphere of the relatively new downtown Boulder pedestrian mall where we walked on cobbled flagstones, licking up Haagen Dazs ice cream cones as we went. With gaping mouths and dripping ice cream, we watched street performers swallow flaming swords.

We spent a couple of days visiting Rocky Mountain National Park, climbing up paved paths to view the majestic mountains in all their splendor. After singing about them for a whole week I felt as if we were already acquainted, but it was exhilarating to finally meet them face to face, to drag my fingers through the sparkling snow that lay on their hillsides in July. The week went by much too fast, and as Uncle Harry and Aunt Di set up chairs for Sunday Fellowship, we loaded the trailer and hugged goodbye.

Dad's plan for the trip home would take us through Nebraska, Iowa, Illinois, Indiana, and back into Michigan. It was a geography lesson I will never forget! Nebraska, especially, will remain forever seared into my mind because that was where the tent finally fell.

The drive home was a bit of a letdown after visiting the exciting sites on the way out to Colorado and the anticipation of reaching the mountains and family. It was a gray, cloudy afternoon when we pulled into a KOA campground that seemed just a bit neglected. We swam in the dingy, above-ground swimming pool until lightning began to streak through the sky. Hurrying out of the pool, we dried off and headed back to the tent as the sky grew darker and darker. The wind began to pick up and as Dad tightened the ropes attached to the tent stakes, Mom folded down the camp chairs we had just set up and then settled Miriam into her playpen for the night.

Reneé and I climbed into our cots, and I tried not to feel nervous about the approaching storm. I had helped our tent survive one deluge already, but would we weather the storm this time? Dad whistled a tune as he battened down the hatches, his clear, confident warble a reassuring sound as I drifted off into a fitful sleep.

Though she spoke quietly, my mom's words a few minutes later woke me instantly. "Frank, I don't like these winds. I'm going to sleep in the van." Immediately I was out of my cot, crying, "Me too!" as I ran for the safety of our solid vehicle. Reneé was right behind me, leaving Simeon and Dad in the tent with Miriam snoring softly in the playpen. All responsibility I had placed on myself to be a good example and a strong helper flew out the unzipped doorway of the tent and away with the wind as I dashed to the van.

I finally, fitfully, dozed off, but it wasn't long before Dad opened the door in a huge gust of wind and with one arm shoved a crying Simeon in with us.

"Take the baby! Take the baby!" he hollered at Mom, handing Miriam to her quickly as rain blew in from behind him. "The *&%# center pole broke, and the tent collapsed on us! I'm gonna throw everything in the trailer and then we'll find a hotel."

Through the window of the van, I tried to follow Dad with my eyes as he made his way through the rain and wind to the tent. I was terrified. Would the wind carry him off? I could see him scooping up the muddy, wet tent and the cots, clothes, and gear inside it in just a few armloads, heaving it all into the little brown trailer and slamming the door. Drenched, he jumped into the van with a few more swear words and drove us to a nearby hotel. After a hurried check-in, we were all sound asleep within minutes, finally safe from the storm.

The next morning, after taking advantage of warm showers and clean towels, we spent hours driving around under a clear blue sky to hardware stores looking to repair or replace the tent pole. Dad showed us the original, which had bent with the ease of a pipe cleaner in the force of the wind and had broken off at one end. We were astonished. Once he had secured a replacement, he emptied the trailer in the parking lot to air out the tent and reorganize our wet and scattered belongings.

After a quick lunch we were back on the road. I was hot and tired and ready to be home; it was hard to keep from whining. Settling into one of the bench seats in the van, I buried my nose in "The Great Brain" borrowed from my cousin and read most of the long, long drive home.

The last leg of the trip was a blur of pavement and roadside parks, until the day we pulled into our driveway in Otsego once again. John Denver was singing, "Hey, it's good to be back home again" on the 8-track, the grass in our front yard was up to my knee, but it was, indeed, good to be back home.

We did not know then that that camping trip would be the last big family trip before our family would change forever.

Later that same summer Mom took me to buy my first bra and, that fall, I entered middle school. The winds of change, beyond my control, were only just beginning to blow.

Chapter 6

...and remember the words of the Lord Jesus,
how He Himself said,
"It is more blessed to give than to receive."

Acts 20:35 ESV

1982

The kids came shortly after I turned twelve. My parents had been taking in newborn foster babies for several years now, taking a break for just a year when Miriam was born. The babies would usually be in our care for only a few months before being adopted–my mom half-joked that just as she got them to sleep through the night they would be given to their permanent family. My parents had begun to seriously consider adopting into our own family.

One warm summer night as I came downstairs to get a drink from the kitchen, I noticed that my dad was awake in the living room, rocking our current baby in the rocking chair. This one was a little girl that we called April. She was groggy and drifting to sleep in his arms. As I came out of the kitchen with my glass, Dad had April up on his shoulder, patting her back and whispering into her tiny ear.

"What are you doing?" I asked, curious. He wasn't singing like Mom would sing to the babies.

Dad chuckled softly.

"Oh, I just like to make sure these kids have information they might need some day, you know, like our telephone number, my social security number, our address... I'm hoping it will sink into her brain and come back to her if she needs us one day." He smiled, almost sheepish.

Honestly, I had never really thought about what happened after the babies left us. Why would they need us?

It wasn't long after that when Dad kept the family around the dining room table one night after dessert.

"Mom and I have been praying about something, and we really think God wants us to do this," he began.

My eyes immediately went to my mom, wanting to gauge her reaction. Dad always seemed to be the one with the grand plans and schemes. She was holding little Miriam, two now, on her lap. And she was smiling–a good sign.

"You know how we've been taking in the foster babies just until they can be adopted?" We all nodded our heads.

"What would you think about adopting someone into our own family?"

Reneé and I looked at each other with excitement. Would we get to keep a sweet, cuddly baby girl like April, who had recently been matched to her forever family?

"We are thinking about adopting a child with a handicap, or maybe a group of brothers and sisters whose parents can't take care of them," Dad said. "It's harder for the agency to find families who will adopt kids in those situations."

Now this sounded different, and more difficult. He had a few pamphlets from the adoption agency on the table for Reneé and I to look over, and I glanced through them thoughtfully. So many faces, kids even my age, who did not have a stable home life. Some of them were handicapped; some pictures showed three or four kids, part of a family hoping to stay together.

It made me pause and consider for the first time what I took for granted. What if Mom and Dad didn't want us? Or were unable to take care of us? What would it be like to be separated from my brother and sisters? I looked up at Dad and nodded my head, agreeing to go along with whatever they decided. What else could I do? How could I say no? Besides, other than the possibility of having to shuffle bedrooms, it sounded fairly simple.

I understood that my parents believed God was calling them to do this, but I couldn't fully comprehend the extent of what that would require. But I didn't question them about it. I just accepted that they knew what they were doing. It was already ingrained in me that anything that had to do with God was good, no question about it.

Over the next weeks we put together a scrap book of pictures, notes, and drawings all about our family so that potential adoptees could get to know who we were. We were soon matched with a sibling group of three–two girls and a boy currently in foster care–and suddenly we were planning a weekend visit.

Their visit to our home would fall just before Christmas. Using my own money, I bought them small gifts from the dime store like Play-Doh, crayons, and Hot Wheels cars. The visit went smoothly; I felt cautious but excited. The little boy had a lot of energy and the girls seemed quiet, almost shy. They really didn't seem any different than other kids I knew. How hard could this be?

If my twelve-year-old self had any reservations, it was too late. The adoption ball kept rolling, and by January they were moving in for good. Seemingly overnight we went from a family of six to a family of nine.

As we walked into the restaurant after the official court hearing where we signed papers and took pictures, heads turned to gape at our large family with all the kids following the hostess to be seated. I could almost see them counting with astonishment in their heads, "5, 6, 7...7 kids??" Two booster seats, extra chairs, more children's menus, and extra crayons. I wasn't sure if I wanted to stand up and defend our enormous family to the onlooking customers or hide behind my menu. Was this how it would be from now on? Was my family now an oddity?

As we headed back to our van after the meal, I hollered, "Stop! Now!" when four-year-old Eric, my new little brother, ran straight into the parking lot, oblivious to the cars pulling in from the busy street. I was carrying my new sister, Kelly, the oldest of the three, on my back in a piggyback ride. "Am I light?" she asked in her squeaky voice, seemingly desperate to not be a burden.

Though I fell naturally into this new role that felt like Assistant Parent, I was feeling a little apprehensive. There was no going back now. So I followed my parents' lead.

As the oldest of this new, larger tribe, I dutifully helped out. I was just old enough to start babysitting, and occasionally my parents would leave me in charge. I liked being the boss, and I liked order. I cherished the thought that my parents considered me responsible.

Not that these were easy times. There were significant adjustments going on for all of us. My three new siblings fell in age between us biological kids, with some overlap. One day I walked into the dining room where my mom was seated at the table, scribbling out a grocery list. Attached to each of her legs was a toddler girl crying out angrily, "MY mommy!" "No, MY mommy!" Mom looked at me with a pained smile.

I wished this wasn't so difficult for my mom; the stress of the transition was changing her. I watched her turn into someone different, someone who had less energy and lost her temper more. I didn't know this mom. Both of my parents, who had always seemed to have all the answers, now at times didn't know what to do. They didn't quite seem to know how to handle the trauma carried by these children born outside of their home.

I battled resentment of my adopted siblings for this, for the tension that now lived in our house along with all these bodies. There was no chance that life would ever go back to the way it was before. I had extraordinarily little control over the situation; there was nothing I could do but roll along.

Would our family be better or worse as a result of the adoption? Or just different forever? Only the future would tell if we'd made a difference.

One night almost a year after the Esper Family Expansion, I lay on the top bunk in the small room I shared with Reneé, now on the main floor after the post-adoption bedroom shuffle. I moaned and cried as the pain in my lower back clenched and loosened relentlessly. Dad turned the light off and, standing at the edge of my bed, rubbed my back gently, staying there until I had cried myself to sleep. The next morning, I discovered I had started my first period.

Even during the hormonal yo-yo years of middle school, I always knew I had a safe place to land in the arms of my parents and our full and noisy home. By late high school, however, I started to feel the winds of restlessness inside and the press of the culture outside. MTV and Madonna beckoned to me from my friends' television sets. I think my parents hoped to keep the world out and Jesus in a little longer, so we didn't own a television through all of my high school years, and for a short time my parents banned listening to the radio on Sundays (bless their hearts). But eventually posters of Prince lined my and Renee's bedroom wall and "Purple Rain" played continuously on our record player.

Comfy as it was, I was tired of being kept in a bubble. My best friend had her driver's license now and we started going to parties where there was alcohol and, of course, boys. The two were not a good combination for me. I slowly entered what felt like a double life–still the responsible and obedient oldest daughter at home but living outside of home in a way that would surely disappoint my parents. At the time I was doing what I believed I had a right to do: make my own choices. At the tender age of 17 it felt heady and empowering.

2005

On November 25, my 36th birthday, Jim and I loaded up our kids and headed to the condo. Jim packed his hair clippers so he could give Dad a haircut, per Mom's request. After overseeing careful hugs for Grandpa, we sent the kids to the basement to play. Jim took out a plastic cape and draped it around Dad's neck, then plugged in the clippers. The radiation treatments on his head had caused Dad's once thick, white mane–that famously likened him to Santa Claus–to begin to fall out, so Jim shaved it close. Mom would trim his beard later.

After the haircut, we enjoyed a moment of levity when Jim pulled a grape Dum Dum sucker from his bag and handed it to Dad.

"You were a good boy during your haircut," he said with a grin.

It was so good to hear my dad chuckle; to see his eyes crinkle as he smiled a genuine smile and popped the sucker in his mouth. There had not been much to laugh about lately, and I thanked God fervently for my gentle and kind husband. I knew this was breaking his heart too. He swept up the hair and then went downstairs to play with the kids for a bit.

This gave me some time to curl up next to Dad on the red couch in front of the fireplace. Mom, ever the giver, hopped up from her seat and returned with wrapped birthday presents for me. She never, ever missed an opportunity for gifts. As she sat back down on the other side of me, I opened them and exclaimed my gratitude. A soft, coral suede blazer. A gravy boat I had been wanting. While they were lovely things, they seemed insignificant compared to the gift of sitting between Mom and Dad one more time.

I was filled with warm flashbacks of lying between them in their bed during thunderstorms in the middle of the night as a child; of riding along with them in the front of the big green van, content to just listen to their conversations; of walking between them on the many walks we would take down our country road. Between them I was safe, I was loved, I was home.

They both wrapped their arms around me and sang "Happy Birthday" softly and sweetly, with Dad slightly out of tune as always. I was hyper aware of the fact that this could be the last time I would hear that song from him. And then the three of us just held each other for a long time, soaking each other in, absorbing one another.

I knew they were carrying an enormous weight inside of them right then. I knew that there were still too many unanswered questions revolving around the C-word and felt a crushing sadness because I was completely powerless to help. I soaked in their love and yet I knew I did not deserve this special attention. They were dealing with something so much more important, more consuming, than me and my little birthday.

But in their giving, I felt them releasing some of that heaviness. Giving is better than receiving–Mom's mantra, always. I wanted so badly to give them hope, to take away their pain; I was angry, still, that I could not fix this for them.

How was it that I got to mark another year of life when my dad most likely would not? Yet there they were, giving to me. All I could do was receive and cherish this tender moment God had given to the three of us.

November 29, 2005

Hi everyone! (Typing corrected by Lynda...)

This is Frank. I wanted to tell you about the very good day I had yesterday.

I got my stitches and big plastic clamps out.

I learned how to get up by myself from a laying position.

My girlfriend and I went out for dinner for the first time.

I had physical therapy.

I had acupuncture therapy.

I feel stronger than I have in weeks.

Mom (my girlfriend) and I watched a fun movie.

I have the energy to come to the keyboard. (Cool, hey?)

Thank you for your love and prayers. God is an excellent provider and is holding us in His arms. Praise Him!!!

Love to all. Should be able to start seeing you in the next 10 days.

Love, Frankie

P.S. Blessings to all from Lynda. We will be in Zeeland from tomorrow until December 11 when we will come back to Zion to start chemo. Don't know what the schedule will be like after that. We are walking with God on this journey, secure in His everlasting love

CHAPTER 7

But while he was still a long way off, his father saw him and felt compassion for him, and ran and embraced him and kissed him.

Luke 15:20 NASB

1983-1990

In Otsego I continued to observe my parents' faith that was growing right along with us kids. Although they seemed to remain wary of organized religion, meaning we still didn't attend any church regularly, the presence of Christ permeated our home.

I knew the Bible was important because my mom had one on her nightstand, with a smooth white leather cover that zipped all the way around. Her notes on the pages were written in small, neat cursive. My dad's Bible was either open on his lap or on the table next to his chair, copious notes in misspelled words scribbled in the margins. I gleaned what little I knew of what they called “The Word” from listening to discussions between my parents from the back of the van or at the dinner table. Somewhere along the way I received a Good News Bible of my own, but only occasionally thumbed through the pages.

Mom had dinner ready every night when Dad got home from work, and he would lead us in prayer before eating. Some nights, especially as our family grew, the chaos of the family table was too much for him after a long day. He would say, “Let’s make tonight a quiet dinner.”

Then, “Lyn? Would you say the prayer?”

The rest of us knew not to talk until we asked to be excused from the table.

Other nights, when he was feeling more jovial and wanted to change things up, my tone-deaf father would lead us in singing something we called “The Song on the Wall” in lieu of dinner-time prayer.

On the dark-paneled wall of the dining room hung a framed Bible verse, Matthew 6:33, printed in calligraphy. In black curly cursive it read, “Seek ye first the kingdom of God, and His righteousness.” The song is that verse set to melody and followed by, “and all these things shall be added unto you; Hallelu, Hallelu...jah!” Though my dad couldn’t carry a tune in a paper bag, he would confidently wave his hands at us, conducting I guess, while we all sang enthusiastically.

This was fun when we were kids, not so much when we were teenagers. But the song–and the verse–is ingrained in my head for eternity.

While I was in middle school, my parents finally settled on a local Methodist church to attend regularly. Dad found a passion for teaching Bible study and Mom found an outlet for serving by sewing and making crafts to sell at the annual Bazaar. My younger siblings got involved in VBS and other activities.

By the time Reneé and I were in high school our parents didn't force us to attend, but one Sunday morning we slid late into the pew while the choir sang slowly and reverently, "Surely...the Lord...is in ... this... place..."

Reneé turned to me and whispered, "Who's Shirley?"

We began to chuckle, which slowly turned into uncontrollable giggling that shook the whole pew. Through the tears of mirth streaming down my face I saw Dad lean over my mother to fix his "saucer eyes" on us, wordlessly warning us to pull ourselves together.

After my laughter subsided and our pastor dug into his sermon, I found myself thinking hard thoughts as I listened while sitting beneath the stained-glass windows.

"I do believe that Jesus is God's Son," I thought to myself, "and that He died on the cross to take away my sin. But what am I supposed to do with that? Where and how does Jesus fit into my world of school and homework and boys?" I never asked these questions out loud, thinking that it was something I should know already and that maybe I was just too ignorant to have understood.

Through my parents' modeling and unspoken teaching, I had cobbled together my own understanding of Christianity, a clear system of "rights" and "wrongs," "do's" and "don'ts." Terms like "grace" and "surrender" were not in my vocabulary yet. And while on the surface I agreed with all the "rights," there was part of me that really, really wanted to participate in the "wrongs." Wasn't it ultimately my choice?

I continued living with one foot in the Christian world in which I was raised and one foot in an exciting new world of choice. The seeds of responsibility and compassion that had been sown into my heart contrasted sharply with the alcohol-laden, rule-breaking search for validation. In the world of choice, I only looked out for me.

By the time I was eighteen, I was living in an apartment with a friend, attending classes at a community college, and working as a waitress. I was barely an adult and though still tethered in some ways to home and my parents, I was employing my free will with abandon.

But grace made me pause when my sister Reneé got pregnant in high school.

She was a senior, a busy cheerleader and in the academic top ten of her class. I was in my second year of community college, preparing to transfer to a university. We both were pushing the boundaries of the way we'd been raised, surrendering to hormones and free will and the press of the world around us. Surrendering to the sweet talk of boys and grasping at their empty promises, promises that seemed much more exciting than the faithful monotony of family, home, and church.

Reneé and I grew up close. After Simeon was born, we became one unit: "The Girls." We were often mistaken for twins, and we looked similar enough that sometimes, just for fun, we let people believe it. Mom would sew or buy matching outfits for us, and we often wore our hair in the same style.

As teens we shared everything from a bedroom to clothes and makeup and once, disastrously, a boyfriend. Technically that was not sharing–I stole him outright. Thankfully the blood of our sisterhood was stronger than fleeting passion; while that boy was forgotten, our bond of friendship only grew stronger.

In high school we shared many Sunday night talks in our tiny yellow bedroom while painting nails and finishing homework. We half-seriously made plans to attend the same university one day, where we would room together and eat bowls of raw chocolate-chip cookie dough to our hearts' content.

But God, in His grace, had other plans to teach us and teach us *well*.

A few months earlier, I had moved back home from my apartment in Kalamazoo to save money before transferring schools; for the first time in my life, I had a tiny bedroom to myself in the basement. Throughout the night before Renee's pregnancy test, I tossed and turned in my bed downstairs. I was terrified, kicking blankets off, sitting up to listen: *Was anyone awake yet? Were Mom and Reneé up doing the test now? Do we know?*

It was as if it were happening to me. It *should've* been happening to me.

I had dutifully remained a virgin all through high school, but my first choice as a graduate was to give that gift away. It was a gift to myself–the gift of choice. It sang its siren song in my ear and in my body, and it opened the door to a world that was exhilarating.

The effects of the choices I made eventually caught up with me, however, in the form of a sexually transmitted disease. It was cleared up with an office visit and medicine, and Mom took care of me but didn't ask too many questions. It was almost as if my parents were too occupied with the rest of the family to worry much about me, as if it was easier to turn a blind eye to my behavior. My teacher was natural consequences; defiant pride kept my shame hidden.

And I knew what Reneé had been doing, who she had been seeing. If she was indeed pregnant, I knew who the father of this baby was. He was a boy battling his own demons; deep down I suspected he would not stick around. And she was so afraid. But in that unspoken sibling pact made to protect our own choices, I never said a word to our parents.

Guilt followed me up the stairs when I finally heard my mom and Reneé moving around, whispering, weeping. Peering around the corner, I saw them embracing outside of the bathroom. Reneé was sobbing, my mom holding her, sad but soothing.

Where was Dad? Did he know?

I continued up more stairs to their bedroom and found him sitting on the edge of their bed, motionless, socks limp in his hand. He turned to me, and I saw tears in his eyes–the first I had ever seen in my life.

"It's positive, isn't it? She's pregnant."

He replied heavily, "Her whole life just changed today."

The sherbet in my punch, a mush of lime green that floated in a pink fizzy liquid, sloshed against the side of my plastic cup as I tilted it up to take a drink. I sat alone with a slice of cake on my lap in the corner of my Aunt Judy's living room and watched quietly as the ladies from church, friends of my parents', and a couple of loyal girlfriends showered Reneé with gifts of baby blankets, booties, and toys. Like my punch, my thoughts were lumpy, sloshing around in my head, fizzy with suspicion yet softened by gratitude.

I was surprised that my sister was being treated so graciously, that no one here seemed upset with her for being pregnant. Through these last eight months I had not heard a word raised against her, I had not heard my parents talk with anger or condemnation. Of course, whispers of gossip floated through conversations with my friends and people from school. Throughout the summer I had heard her crying at night, overwhelmed with thoughts of the future.

But the consequence of her choices, which roundly protruded from beneath her maternity dress, was being covered over at this baby shower with loving words, coos of matronly advice, and humorous labor and delivery stories. What I saw before me was love, acceptance.

Mercy over judgment.

This extravagant scene of grace and kindness spoke volumes to my searching soul. I found myself wondering where, how, and even *if* I fit into this picture. I continued in my sin, unhindered by previous consequences, not altered even by my sister's predicament. My sin, unlike Renee's, was hidden, tucked away from sight.

Would these women have had this same kind of grace for me if they knew? The fruit of my sin was not a cute and cuddly baby–redemption in a diaper–but HPV, drunkenness, promiscuity; not to mention a cheapened and dirtied self-image. I was broken, used, all in the name of choice. Could I ever be "eligible" for grace like this?

1991

After I transferred to Central Michigan University, God remained always in the back of my mind. His love was etched in my heart and mind, but I treated Him like a devoted sidekick that I could bring out only when needed for my own benefit.

I engaged in vivid self-talk one day as I vacuumed our dorm room, attacking the carpet viciously, hoping to suck away the conflict in my head. I seemed to argue daily with this critical voice that flooded my mind. It chastised me yet again for my behavior, trying to convince me I was disappointing *someone*. I didn't know who this voice was or where it came from. Was it my conscience? Was it the voice of exacting expectations that I had placed upon myself?

Suspecting it might be God chastising me, I found myself thinking, "Look, God, I know you are there. And I believe you are God. But I am going to live my life the way

I want to live it. Now leave me alone." I left my sidekick on the side of the road and continued down my own path, alone.

But a year or so later, on a dark night in the spring, I found myself alone at my desk in the dorm. I was bummed because Jim, my new boyfriend, was playing in a hockey game and I had too much homework to be able to go. My roommate was at a sorority meeting and the room was quiet, but I was feeling too distracted to focus on my textbook. Something was unsettled inside me, a gnawing feeling of emptiness, a feeling that had not left me alone in recent days.

My eyes fell upon a sweet note from Jim on my desk, reminding me how lucky I was to be dating a guy who genuinely loved me and was treating me better than any boyfriend anywhere, ever. I should have felt so content!

Not only did I have a steady boyfriend, but my education was progressing smoothly. I had been admitted to the school of education at CMU and was preparing to be a teacher. I was 21 years old and the pieces of my life seemed to be falling into place. Why did I feel like something was missing?

As the words on the page in front of me started to blur, I lifted my eyes to let them roam around my room again. They fell upon the Bible tucked into the crate that held my books. It was the Bible that was given to me by my parents for my 13th birthday. I had thrown it in at the last minute as I packed for school, more out a sense of duty, maybe even for show, than any real desire to read it.

I sighed as I realized this faith of mine was like a favorite worn stuffed animal that kept turning up in my life after

I had tried to keep it hidden, always requiring me to do something with it whether I wanted to or not. I would not come out and deny its existence, but this ragged yet special possession kept cluttering the closet of my mind. I could push the dusty thing aside, stuff it underneath my bed or to the very back of my closet, but it would still be there. *Maybe,* I thought, *it's time to do something with it once and for all.*

I pushed aside my Child Development textbook and pulled the Bible in front of me. "Okay, Lord, what do you want to say to me?" I felt both wary and defiant. I had almost zero Bible knowledge. Up to this point in my life all things related to God had been *felt,* intuitive, emotional. Observed and absorbed. What did the Bible actually *say*? Did I really want to know?

Over the last few weeks there had been evenings when I opened my Bible and began to read, searching for *something*... only to slam the Bible shut at the first nudge of conviction. Sure enough, as I started flipping pages this time a confusing mix of phrases that sounded like harsh rules jumped out at me. They felt like accusations.

But this time ... this time I also saw words like redeem, rescue, restore. Some words were familiar, like Psalm 23 and the story of Jesus' birth. I skimmed over words about sexual sin and "fornication" and inwardly groaned, my cheeks warming as I imagined God seeing everything I had done over the last several years. How could He love someone like me after all the ways I had put my own desires before anything (and anyone) else?

I lifted my head and closed my eyes. I did not fit into the picture of holiness that I saw in those pages at all! There were some high standards to meet here. I had broken in some way every commandment or call to right living I came across–if not by my actions, then by thoughts in my heart.

And then I stumbled across Isaiah 30:18-21 (NIV):

Yet the Lord longs to be gracious to you; therefore He will rise up to show you compassion. For the Lord is a God of justice; blessed are all who wait for him! O people ... you will weep no more. How gracious He will be when you cry for help! As soon as He hears, He will answer you. Although the Lord gives you the bread of adversity and the water of affliction, your teachers will be hidden no more; with your own eyes you will see them. Whether you turn to the right or to the left, your ears will hear a voice behind you, saying, "This is the way; walk in it."

Although it would be years before I could read and understand this verse in its larger context, the words spoke loudly and lovingly to me that night. Was I calling for help? *Yes. Yes, I was.*

The phrases "He longs to be gracious" and "He will rise up to show you compassion" conjured up images of the baby shower for Reneé, an unwed pregnant teenager on the receiving end of grace. Her sin was obvious, yet God's mercy poured out on her like a flood. Not only had He added joy upon joy to the Esper family in the form of her newborn son, His mercy had given her a newfound freedom and confidence. He had transformed her. Could this same kind of grace really be for me, too? It was more than I could comprehend. Suddenly the thought of walking down a straight path with a voice behind me saying "This is the way," filled my heart with peace.

I realized I was tired, so tired of trying to determine right from wrong on my own; making excuses in order to appease my own selfishness. I was tired of trying to be two people at once: the responsible student, daughter, and sister in a loving family, and the wild party girl who went along with anything to find approval in the world. For years I had lived in the muddy middle, rebelling against what I knew in my heart–yet denied–was God's desire to protect me and draw me to Him. The security I so longed for had been available to me all along, and though I had glimpses of it in my family and now in my sweet Jim, I had been stubbornly refusing God's free gift of ultimate security–Himself.

I felt a conviction that everything that had shaped me up to this point, even when I pushed it aside to be my own boss, was true and real, and it was my choice to believe it. And if I chose to believe it, I had to choose to live it.

From that moment on, I knew that I could no longer keep my faith as a separate entity that I shoved to the dark and dusty corners of my mind. Though I was heartbroken by my sinfulness as reflected in the Bible, I was filled with hope at the promise of forgiveness, freedom, and new life in Christ.

I felt clumsy and not a little awkward as I got up from my desk chair and knelt upon the carpet remnant on my dorm room floor. Lying prostrate, tears flowing, I mumbled my confession–my willful, sinful past, all of which He already knew, through which He loved me anyway–and I was overwhelmed and humbled. His grace washed over me, leaving me free of the shame, the uncertainty, the wrestling. My faith was real, my Savior more real still, and I had made the choice to embrace Him. I was a new creation.

The next day I taped a yellow, lined piece of notebook paper with Isaiah 30:18-21 written on it to the mirror above my dresser. I breathlessly shared my experience with Jim and while he seemed slightly wary, unsure of what this meant exactly, he was not completely surprised. We had had conversations about God before. But he was supportive of me and, surprisingly, agreed to start attending a local church with me.

Over the weekend I called home to share the news with my parents.

"Good morning!" As always, Dad answered the phone cheerfully, though Caller ID was still a thing of the future.

"Dad! I ... I decided to follow Jesus, I guess!" I laughed, unsure of the proper terminology. "I prayed the other night and I really want to live as a Christian!"

"Well, Cher..." I heard his voice catch. "Wow. That is somethin'. Really." He seemed surprised but moved.

As I chattered, he dug out his Bible. I could hear the pages rustling.

"You know," he said, "I'm thinking of the parable in Luke, the one about the lost sheep? Where Jesus says, 'There will be more joy in heaven over one sinner who repents than over ninety-nine righteous persons who need no repentance.'" He paused. "The angels are rejoicing, Cher." Again, I heard his voice catch with emotion.

He went on to read a couple more passages from Luke 15 to me. Each parable in this chapter was about something lost being found: a lost sheep, a lost coin, a lost son.

As I listened, I saw in the prodigal son's father both my earthly father and my heavenly Father, with arms wide open welcoming me. I didn't feel different, but I knew that something different had happened.

I had been found, and I was welcomed.

2005

After a quiet Thanksgiving at home, Mom and Dad made the trip back to Zion for just a few more days of PT, radiation, meetings, bloodwork, and even acupuncture. Our prayers were now focused on an upcoming PET scan scheduled for early December, specifically asking that it would either show the primary source of his cancer–which could then be surgically removed and/or treated–or that the cancer had not spread anymore. Though I prayed "Your will be done, Lord," what I really wanted was my will–that the cancer would all just go away. My words were submissive but my heart was reckless, desperate.

The day after this scan, back in Michigan, Dad insisted on attending Esper Electric's annual Christmas party. He had lost so much weight that he had to wear suspenders to hold his pants up, but he proudly donned his Team Esper baseball cap over his now bald head. He and Mom climbed into Miriam's minivan, allowing her to be their chauffeur for the evening.

While Dad and Mike had forged a strong partnership that made Esper Electric successful as a business, it was Dad and Mom's partnership that made it feel like a family. Mom used her creative generosity to host a large party each summer in their backyard for the Esper employees and their families, ordering steaks for grilling and games and prizes for the kids. Dad made sure the pool was sparkling and would set up a volleyball or badminton net in the yard. At Christmas time they hosted a nice dinner for the adults, usually at an upscale hotel so that those who might choose to overindulge in celebration could safely spend the night.

This year's Christmas party was bittersweet. Through the colorful Christmas lights and sparkling champagne, Miriam keenly observed the way Dad let himself be led around the room. He shook everyone's hand and asked about their children by name. She noticed his tired eyes twinkling as he listened intently to the latest updates, genuine care for his employees and their families radiating from him. It seemed that for just a few hours he was able to forget about cancer; he was the Captain of Team Esper again, talking shop and hugging his employees for whom he had such great affection.

A few days later, we received the results of the PET scan.

Dad's team of doctors had finally discovered the root of the cancer in his esophagus. Locating the primary source sounded like such a great victory; Mom and Dad were cautiously optimistic about now treating this Mother Weed that had spread so aggressively throughout his body. Chemo began immediately back in Zion, and the doctors even began to tentatively discuss the option of surgery on the brain tumors–if they could confirm that they had indeed stopped growing.

By the week before Christmas, they were home again in Michigan for a reprieve from treatment. Despite their hope, the treatments were terribly hard on Dad. We planned our usual Christmas family get-together at the condo, but that morning I called my mom in tears.

"I don't know what to do, Mom," I wailed. "I have a terrible cold, and Levi and Audrey have runny noses. Should we be around Dad?"

Mom had held her hope loosely as she watched Dad suffer the side effects of chemo.

"Honey, this will probably be his last Christmas with us. I think you should come," she said gently.

Dad sat in his walker with a mask on. He was extremely wiped out from the chemo, his body weak and his heart heavy. He did not speak much. I hid behind the noise and excitement of the kids as we exchanged gifts; it was a veil to cover the profound depth of my sadness.

Was Mom right? Would this be our last Christmas with Dad? Could he come out of this and recover? Could there be a miracle in his future when things looked so bleak, even beneath the twinkling lights of the Christmas tree?

I was still trying to control the rest of my life and do everything right, including Christmas. As I did every year, I found myself thinking, "This year my kids are going to get a new perspective on Christmas. This year we are going to help more people, give more money, and tell more people that Christmas is about Jesus. This year–really–we will get the kids fewer gifts and teach them about being content with what they have. This year we will celebrate Advent, we'll light the candles, we'll read the Scriptures, we'll do all the good things." Inevitably, at the end of every Christmas season, I would sigh and think, "We could've done it better."

But one day while Jim and I were doing our Christmas planning, I walked into our family room to discover one of Levi's dingy, white gym socks hung from a nail above the fireplace. Our five-year-old just could not wait for the fancy stockings, handmade by Grandma Esper, that we usually hung a couple days before Christmas. He was ready to receive! While I laughed outright at the sight and promptly took a picture, I contemplated this visual representation of innocent faith.

Why did I need a fancy stocking or to do everything "right" to receive the free gifts–THE gift–God had for me? Did it change the truth that God had sent his Son to rescue me? This year, of all years, while physical death was a near and consuming reality, I should have been contemplating the real gift that the birth of Jesus brought. He was born to die so that eternal life could be given to those whose bodies would perish. All anyone had to do was receive it.

Though the healing miracle I sought under the Christmas tree lights did not seem to be forthcoming, my son's dirty gym sock reminded me that hope–the promise of eternal life–was the real gift.

When God found me in my dorm room and poured out His forgiveness for my past and grace for my future, assuring me of hope both for this life on earth and for the life to come, I had received this gift.

And I reminded myself that this hope was for my dad, too, no matter what happened next.

CHAPTER 8

When the earth totters, and all its inhabitants,
it is I who keep steady its pillars.

Psalm 75:3 ESV

1992

I hung up the phone with Reneé after having one last cry together and finished packing my suitcase. The rehearsal dinner was over, everyone was in bed, and the next day I would marry Jim, this man that I loved so much...and then we would move 500 miles away. I put on my pajamas and brushed my teeth, but there was one more thing I needed to do.

I climbed the stairs to my parents' room, where they breathed in the air of dreams. Quietly I slipped under my dad's arm on their bed, careful not to wake Mom.

"Dad?" I whispered.

"Huh? Oh, hi honey," he chuckled. "What are you doing?"

"I'm getting married tomorrow. Can you believe it?" I laughed, giddy with nerves.

"Oh yeah. I can," Dad said sleepily. A long pause. His eyes had not opened, but then he shifted. "Jim's a good guy. He's gonna take real good care of you. I'm so happy." He patted me reassuringly.

"Me too." I snuggled closer to Dad. His confidence in Jim, and me, and the two of us as a unit, transferred to my skin in the strength of his arm around me.

"Tomorrow's gonna be a fun day," he said "You kids are gonna do alright."

"Yeah?" I asked.

"... Yeah."

Mom murmured something unintelligible, and I took that as her vote of confidence, too.

"Dad?" I asked again.

"Huhhhh...?" he said sleepily.

"You are my sunshine, my only sunshine..." I sang softly the words he used to sing to me as a little girl.

"...You make me happyyyyy when skies are gray..." he responded, his voice whispery and warbling. I felt his whiskered cheeks move into a grin.

His breathing was getting heavier, I knew he was falling back to sleep.

I lay there a few minutes longer under his arm–the closing parenthesis of my childhood. My stomach fluttered with excitement as I thought about walking down the aisle on that arm in just a few hours, wearing the gorgeous dress my mom had spent all summer sewing.

The little apartment up north was waiting for Jim and me, as husband and wife, and so were the next chapters of my life. I smiled in the darkness.

I kissed Dad softly on the cheek and slipped out of the bed.

"Good night, Daddy."

1995 - 1998

Dear Dad,

Happy 50th Birthday! We love you and are excited to tell you that your birthday present will be arriving in about nine months!

Love,
Jim and Cheryl

Jim and I crossed the gravel parking lot under the hot July sun and walked into the Italian restaurant just down the road from Esper Electric. The surprise birthday party Mom had thrown Dad was already in full swing. Dad greeted us with a huge grin and flaunted the AARP card he had received in the mail that morning.

"Look at this! I'm officially a senior citizen!" he laughed.

We hugged and Jim and I wished him a happy birthday, handing him the card from us. I was so excited for him to open it that my stomach was in knots. Mom came over for a hug too; she didn't know our news yet either, and I was trembling with the anticipation of their reaction.

But my dad, Mr. Social, "Uncle Frank" to everybody, took his time walking around, greeting everyone with a handshake and a hug, introducing us to people we hadn't met before. Jim and I found a booth along the side of the reserved room, and finally my parents joined us there.

"Are you going to open your card from us?" I asked Dad.

"Oh! Yeah. You want me to open it now?"

"Yes!"

He pulled it from his back pocket and slid his finger underneath the sealed flap of the envelope.

I was dying of excitement inside and I burst into giggles of glee when Dad's saucer eyes appeared over the top of the card, his mouth a round "oh" of surprise.

"You're gonna have a baby?" he said. He was grinning from ear to ear, looking back and forth between Jim and me. "Whadaya know! Congratulations, honey! And you too, Jimbo!" he stretched his hand across the table to clasp Jim's, his eyes shining.

Mom was smiling too, with a knowing look. Hmm, maybe she had been picking up on hints that I didn't know I was dropping. We stood up and she squeezed me tight.

"I'm so excited for you," she said warmly.

The birth of our son, Jared Keith, took my faith to a whole new level. As I sat in our bedroom on the night we brought him home, holding this sleeping baby in my arms, I was overwhelmed with the love flowing through me. I knew that there was *nothing* this child could do to make me not love him.

And I was struck suddenly by the thought that this, *this*, is how God loved me, *His* child! I was amazed and profoundly humbled. I had tasted a morsel of this miraculous love when I came face to face with the Lord years earlier, but now I was holding in my arms a living, breathing picture of God's love for me.

Our second child, Courtney Renee, came about two and a half years later and was a little peanut of a baby. Her birth was the happy ending to fifteen hours of hard labor, and never was a full head of dark hair such a joyous sight. But the day of her birth brought the sound of a heart murmur. The pediatrician said, "Don't worry, most heart murmurs are gone within twenty-four hours."

Hers was not.

Our tiny baby girl was hooked up to an echocardiogram machine in the hospital nursery, and as I prayed and cried and my milk came in, the doctors found a hole in the middle of her heart. The gentle cardiologist explained to us that walls that were supposed to be there were not formed correctly, and blood-flow-regulating valves were not doing their job. Surgery would correct these issues, but not for another six months.

"Take her home and let her grow and get stronger, she will be fine until then," he told us.

We took her home.

Oh, how my babies screamed! Those first two, Jared and Courtney, were my criers. Late nights pacing by the light of the aquarium with our newborn son two years earlier girded our loins for the screaming of our daughter.

As I walked her up and down our apartment floor by night, we waited by day for a closing date on our shoebox of a first home. Though I repeatedly insisted towards the end of my pregnancy that I WOULD NOT BE MOVING WITH A BRAND-NEW BABY, in September we moved into the house with a brand-new baby. Jim and I now paced the shag-covered, creaking floors of our "new" 1940s ranch with this banshee, passing her back and forth to each other so we could sleep in between shifts, tag-teaming in the care of our busy and inquisitive two-year-old son.

After living in the Upper Peninsula for the first year of our marriage, we had moved back to Portage, right next to Kalamazoo, and had found a church home right around the corner. We made friends our age and attended Bible study; together Jim and I were baptized in December 1993.

When Jared was a toddler, God used my church mamas to encourage me to grow my faith, which was enthusiastic but still uninformed at that point. My relationship with God was still mostly based on emotion, snippets of Scripture preached from the pulpit, and a ton of previous parental influence.

But these dear mother hens would not stop inviting me to Bible Study Fellowship, they loved me so much. And I finally went, even though it meant paying one of the high school girls from church to babysit on Monday nights; Jim was coaching youth hockey after work so we could pay the bills.

BSF was a feast for my soul, taking all the pieces of Scripture I had absorbed through the years and stitching them into a bigger, beautiful story. God's Word finally began to come to life for me, and these godly women surrounded me with love, grace, and example.

By the time Courtney was born and we had moved into our home in Kalamazoo, I was in my second year of BSF and training to be a discussion group leader. This meant that I was required to attend (early) Saturday morning meetings each week in preparation for Monday's class. I would wake before the sun, nurse Courtney, hand her over to Jim, usually fussy, (Courtney, not Jim. Well, sometimes Jim) and head to the church for the meeting. It was a balm to me, even as exhausted as I was. I was being taught truth, shown love, and modeled how to pray in a way that infused life and energy into this fatigued young mother.

And in that tired, worried year, the Lord loved me and carried me through His good Word and His godly women. These sisters, these prayer warriors, as well as our church people and blood family, covered my little family in prayer as we approached Courtney's heart surgery.

We arrived at C.S. Mott Children's Hospital on the University of Michigan's campus prayed up full and with eyes wide open for a miracle. We were ready to tell even the bell hop that we were here for a reason, and it was to share God with everyone we met.

But even as our tiny pink piglet of a baby girl smiled at passing nurses and doctors, our balloon of hope was soon deflated. The pre-surgery echocardiogram revealed more issues than just the faulty valves and hole in Courtney's heart. The doctors determined that Courtney had Pulmonary Artery Stenosis, a narrowing of arteries not discovered in the early echocardiogram on the day of her birth; a different plan for surgery would be required.

The pictures from the echo that we were convinced would show a miraculously healed, beating baby heart–and that would tell us to pack our bags and head back home with great rejoicing–instead informed us that this was just the beginning of a longer, more complicated road.

We traveled back to Kalamazoo not with a miracle but with a re-scheduled surgery and many questions:

Didn't we do everything we were supposed to do? We trusted God, we prayed, we even had the elders at church anoint our baby with oil and pray over her. Why, God? What did we do wrong?

As I studied the Psalms in BSF, that book of the Bible became a soft place for me to land. I cried out to God with the Psalmists in anguish, with these questions and more, and even demands. Like David, I was able to dry my tears on the hope of God's promises, trusting that He was worthy of praise despite any outcome, desired or not; despite prayers answered or unanswered.

I had no other hope.

Surgery was smooth but long. Infused with relief after hearing the operation was successful and our little girl was doing fine, I finally accepted that *this* was God's healing. It didn't look the way I thought or even wanted it to look. But it was healing, it was success, and we were ready to grow into a future of normalcy.

While our girl, puffy from meds and connected to a million tiny wires, lay sedated in her diaper in the NICU, a random pediatrician on rotation (who forever in my mind will have the bedside manner of Napoleon Dynamite) first mentioned Williams Syndrome to us.

"Courtney seems to have some of the characteristics of this syndrome," he said, handing me a photocopy of a page of words from a textbook. "We'll run a test and let you know." I scanned the two paragraphs of information quickly and handed it to Jim. This was not our daughter. It couldn't be. Those paragraphs described a future of constant health issues, anxiety, learning disabilities. Our daughter was a tiny little fighter, her life on the mend already.

I dismissed it immediately. We had had our speed bump, and now it was time to move on.

I called my parents that night and, after talking to Jared, whose voice and cuddles I missed with an ache in my chest, I asked Dad to look up Williams Syndrome on the World Wide Web. An amazing recent invention, the internet was clearly more sophisticated than a single textbook page, and it would surely confirm that this syndrome was not something that should concern us. Dad reported back the next day that he couldn't find anything about Williams Syndrome on the internet.

Only later would I learn he had been trying to protect me, to shield me from more information than I needed in that moment.

We became happily distracted when the nurse told us after three days we could *finally* hold our daughter. Courtney didn't seem excited to eat, not even my own breastmilk from a bottle, dutifully pumped every day. Finally she was moved from NICU to a recovery room, she began eating, to our joy, and then at long last we signed her release papers so we could go home.

One week after the operation, we drove determinedly through a Michigan blizzard to get home to normalcy, to our little boy's third birthday, to After Surgery.

The piano and organ blended together soothingly in the prelude to worship. People were still filing into the auditorium in the few minutes before church started. Jared was in his preschool class and Courtney was in the nursery. I sat down beside Jim and with a shaky hand I grabbed a roll-call card from the rack before me. My heart pounded and my brain was on overdrive, overwhelmed by looming news. We were still waiting for the results of the FISH test that Dr. Loker, the pediatric cardiologist, had ordered after Courtney's last check-up.

Courtney had recovered well from her heart surgery and was now a chunky eight-month-old with a ton of hair that I loved to adorn with colorful bows and headbands. Dr. Napoleon Dynamite's cold suggestion that Courtney could have Williams Syndrome had been shoved to the very back of my mind during her recovery and getting settled back at home. I just wanted to get back to normal as soon as possible.

Since we'd been home, however, my baby girl had become a nightmarish nurser. When I had stopped breastfeeding Jared after six months, he had immediately developed a string of chronic ear infections, so I was determined to nurse

Courtney for a full year. But shortly after surgery, when I would settle in to nurse her, she would pull at my nipple and turn her head away from me while nursing, as if it was a rubber pacifier she could chew on. It was excruciating and we were both miserable.

Though I had pumped daily while she recovered from surgery at the hospital, I wondered if there was a problem with my milk supply. I consulted a local breastfeeding specialist who admitted she had never seen anything like this; she suggested I begin supplementing with formula. I hated to do it, knowing how good a mother's milk is for her baby. But I did, both for her health and my sanity, and Courtney quickly began to gain some much-needed weight.

She did not, however, show any signs of rolling over or enough strength to sit up by herself. At a little over eight months old, she slouched over in her highchair and Exersaucer, her feet swishing back and forth on the bottom.

When Jim and I took her to her cardiologist for the two -month post-op visit, Dr. Loker was surprised at her lack of development. He thoughtfully flipped through her chart, consulting the information sent over from the hospital in Ann Arbor regarding her heart surgery. Then he glanced up at us.

"You ever get the results of the FISH test?" he asked, looking over his glasses at me.

"Her what?" I asked. I tickled Courtney's tummy as she lay on her back on the examination table, and she kicked her feet at me in delight. She had been slow to smile as an infant; we told people she smiled with her feet.

"It says here they requested a FISH test, a test for Williams Syndrome, but I can't tell if they ever ran one. FISH stands for *fluorescent in situ hybridization*, it's a genetic test. Did you ever get any results?"

Jim and I looked at each other.

"No, we didn't," Jim said. "It was mentioned one time at the hospital, but then nothing was ever said about it again."

"Hm. Well, I'm gonna order that to be done here. I don't see any results in her chart, and I have a suspicion..."

He went on to explain that in our DNA, each numbered chromosome comes in a pair, from 1 to 23. In people with Williams Syndrome, a FISH test reveals that a small portion of genetic material on one of the number seven chromosomes is missing; it happens in about 1 in every 10,000 births. These people share distinct facial features like puffy eyes and a small chin, small stature, low muscle tone, and pinky fingers and toes that curl in. And, more seriously, cardiovascular defects, learning deficiencies, and other possible health concerns. Dr. Loker mentioned he had treated a few patients with Williams Syndrome, and now that Courtney was older, he could see some of the characteristics of it in her. Especially since she was showing some gross-motor delays.

He handed us a stack of information about Williams Syndrome to read, just in case, and sent us down to the lab to get blood drawn from Courtney for the test. All the way home I pored over the papers Dr. Loker had given us. Included in the stack was a thick newsletter from the Williams Syndrome Association that happened to be based in Michigan. The reader in me couldn't take it in fast enough, though a voice in my head was shouting, "Slow down! You don't even know yet if this pertains to you! Don't overdo it! You're just going to get upset!" But I was immersed in the literature, my heart going from zero to Worst Case Scenario in 60 seconds flat.

In church that day, all the information I devoured from those papers was swimming in my head. I was convinced my daughter had a *syndrome*, and I was already in mourning. The people closest to me knew that something was going on, that there might be more going on with our baby girl than just a heart defect. That morning they murmured questions and concerns to me, they told me they were praying for us. The future blurred before me and I could hardly catch my breath.

I looked down to where I had signed the roll call card only to realize I had written, "Jim and Cheryl Syndrome." I burst into tears.

Two days later we received a phone call from Dr. Loker. He had positively diagnosed our baby girl with Williams Syndrome.

2006

I have never been good at holding the unknown in my hands. I am the type of person who wants to know what to expect, to know what the plan is, to know how to prepare.

At this point in my life there are more unknowns than just whether or not my Dad will live or die.

There was such joy and anticipation when Jim and I were first married; when the future lay long and bright before us, it was easy to have hope. There was lots of room for change.

There was joy in the waiting for the birth of a child, even in not knowing whether that child would be a boy or a girl. When I was younger the unknown held promise for me, my mind only envisioning–only allowing–beautiful outcomes.

Now Jim and I have four young children and our daughter with challenges has allowed us to see that not a single one of their futures is guaranteed. When you have experienced a painful outcome, not the thing you were expecting, the next unknown can become agonizing.

January brings nothing but cold and chemo. Mom finally catches up on her own care, going to re-scheduled dentist and hair appointments while their roller-coaster car coasts on a plateau. My parents travel to the CTCA in Zion just once for a couple rounds of treatment, but Dad is only getting weaker. Back in Michigan, a visit to the emergency room reveals that some of the medication Dad is taking is causing more problems. An MRI is scheduled for the end of the month to determine what, if any, progress is being made.

My parents have lots of visitors. Their friends John and Diane, and Craig and Lorna, are constantly checking in with phone calls, bringing food and wine. Relatives they haven't seen in a while are starting to show up. People know this is serious.

My brother Eric flies in from Kansas. Five years earlier, he had reconciled with Mom and Dad after many difficult years of being estranged; he expresses great love and gratitude for our parents. Our sister Kelly visits often and thoughtfully pours out her heart to Dad in a letter, thanking him for changing the trajectory of her life. Each of them is living proof of God's faithfulness and healing grace, despite mistakes made in our human family. Though there are still some painful, residual injuries for everyone related to the adoption, God's healing hand is at work in us all.

In the middle of the month Jim and the kids drive me to the train station in downtown Kalamazoo. After lots of hugs and kisses and waves through the window, I settle in my seat with a good book for the ride to Chicago.

Our amazing husbands Jim and Pete had gotten together and planned a shopping weekend for Reneé and I in the Windy City as a Christmas gift. I will take the train to Union Station and Reneé will drive down through Wisconsin from their home in the western U.P. to meet me at our hotel.

My sister and I share about a million private jokes. A single word can produce gales of laughter; the name of someone from long ago can bring forth a story rehashed over and over again, sometimes with laughter and sometimes with tears. We finish each other's sentences and complete each other's memories.

Laughter is a gift from God that allows us to release pent up feelings; it is as powerful and cleansing as tears. And in this current season filled with both the busyness of family and the dark cloud of cancer hanging over us all, I am hungry for it.

But laughter is a quandary for me these days.

One of the many challenges for kids with Williams Syndrome is extremely sensitive hearing–hyperacusis. Certain sounds, especially if unexpected, can produce physical pain in Courtney's ears. Anxiety is another all-consuming facet of Williams Syndrome, and so a noise that causes pain also brings extreme anxiety in the anticipation of it happening again.

For example, a single cloud in the sky brings a hundred repetitions of "Is it going to storm today?" leading Courtney to lay on the couch, rock her head from side to side and moan sadly, "I just want the sky to cheer up!"

For reasons we will never understand, laughter is a double-sided demon for Courtney, particularly the sound of *my* laughter. She is eight now; she was four when we really began to notice how certain sounds were affecting her. In addition, her anticipation anxiety has become exhausting for all of us.

Reneé and I talk on the phone at least once, if not twice, a day. And whenever we do, laughter is inevitable. But I have learned in recent years to shut myself in the bathroom if a giggle makes its way into my throat. I've learned to swallow my laughter and cover my mouth if Courtney is in the room because her radar goes up the minute she knows who I'm talking to.

"Oh noooo, not Aunt Reneé!" she will wail. Then, "What's so funny, Mom? Why did you slap your thigh? Was it funny? Why are your shoulders shaking?"

I am under a microscope, and though she tries to hold it in Courtney just cannot tolerate the irritation and distress. Suddenly her hands will go up over her ears and a scream will erupt from her mouth. Not only is she in pain, but she is angry.

Kind of ruins the mood, doesn't it?

I arrive at our hotel room first, and Reneé calls me from her cell to tell me she's in the parking garage.

When I open the door to her knock, we squeal and hug each other tightly. It is so good to see her. We've seen each other quite a bit this past fall, but always in the context of the hospital in Zion or at Mom and Dad's. Reneé is a high-school math teacher and has taken time off to be with our parents; we all have. Though Tyler is sixteen now, Pete and Reneé have had two more children who are three and one. She is grateful for this weekend away, too.

She releases me from her hug, places her hands on my shoulders and looks me directly in the eye, sighing deeply. "You know I love our parents."

"Of course!" I reply. "Why do you say that?"

"I think we need to make a pact to not talk about Dad this weekend." Her voice cracks as she says this, and I feel tears sting in my own eyes. But I completely understand. Nothing we can say or discuss this weekend is going to change anything at the moment. We both need a break. The weight of grief and worry are not allowed on this trip.

Though this in-between place of not knowing what the future holds–for both my dad and my daughter–is a constant residence for me, this weekend I leave it behind. And it is glorious. I enjoy shopping with my best friend in the whole world, away from responsibilities, kids, dirty dishes, and laundry. Just for a couple of days I manage to slide out from underneath the aura of mourning, laughing as hard as I want without feeling guilty for causing anyone pain.

It's much-needed grace in the grieving, fresh air blown from the hand of God. He is teaching me to rest in Him.

Chapter 9

So we fix our eyes not on what is seen,
but on what is unseen,
since what is seen is temporary,
but what is unseen is eternal.

2 Corinthians 4:18 NIV

February 2006

Saturday, February 11, 2006

Dear Family and Friends,

This has probably been one of the hardest weeks Lynda and I have had to face.

1 – We met with the neurosurgeon (brain surgeon) on Tuesday. He does not think that the brain cancer as it stands is operable, so he ordered two tests to check the stats of the growth of the rest of my cancer.

2 – I failed the tests miserably ... and, we found a very serious blood clot near my chemo port, in my major artery.

3 – We went to the hospital Thursday and Friday, inpatient, and met with a surgeon to see if we could remove the clot. No deal–too dangerous. So, we're home, on blood-thinners to stabilize the clot. The danger involved with blood thinners is bleeding of the brain tumors.

God is still with us. Please continue to pray for us as we struggle through these times. All of our love and prayers are with you. Frank and Lynda

P.S. We'd like to share with you a portion of a prayer taken from a book entitled "31 Days of Praise" by Ruth Myers:

All that I am and all that I have I give to You. I give You my body and each of its members...my entire inner being; my mind, my emotional life, my will ... my loved ones ... my marriage ... my abilities and gifts...my strengths and weaknesses ... my health...my status (high or low) ...my possessions...my past, my present, and my future...when and how I'll go Home.

I'm here to love You, to obey You, to glorify You. O my Beloved, may I be a joy to You!

Snowflakes fall softly as I drive down the lamp-lit streets through the dark morning. It's Friday, and I'm on my way to Holland General Hospital. I stop and go behind a lumbering yellow bus as it picks up children for school.

I spent last night at the condo, while Mom spent the night at the hospital with Dad. I promised I would relieve her around 7 a.m., and so after sending an email update to my church family, whose prayers have been vital and faithful, I head out into the early morning.

I'm not sure what the day will hold after receiving news of the precarious, nefarious blood clot yesterday. I send up a prayer as I drive, asking God to empty me of all expectations and prepare me to listen, love, and help today.

Beside me is a bag with note cards and a list of people who have been on my mind lately, and I will write cards as I sit with Dad. One of Mom's repeated phrases to us as we were growing up was, "The best thing to do when you are feeling down is something for someone else." I will put this into practice as I sit and do battle with grief again today.

Little House on the Prairie is on the TV in Dad's hospital room when I walk in. I hug my tired mom and send her on her way for sleep and a shower.

As we watch the show absentmindedly, I am eight years old again. I'm lying next to Dad on the blue shag carpet in the living room, watching this very show with the family on a tiny black and white TV. We're eating popcorn made in the hot-air popper and I can practically taste the Kraft parmesan cheese sprinkled on top.

When it goes to commercial, Dad turns the volume down and sighs as I settle in next to him and open the Bible on my lap. We make small talk and I read a couple of psalms to him.

I have been spending a lot of time in the book of Psalms the last few months. As they did when we were preparing for Courtney's heart surgery and in the early years after her diagnosis, they provide comfort and reassurance. They remind me that there is nothing that God does not see or know about, there is nothing out of His realm of control, and there is nothing we can't cry out to Him about. And they remind me that He is ever-present, even on hard days like today.

I have recently been meditating on Psalm 119:50: "My comfort in my suffering is this: your promise preserves my life." I share this with Dad, but he is quiet.

"You know they found a blood clot near my heart," he finally says after a few minutes of silence.

I put my Bible aside and take his hand. "Yeah, that's what Mom said."

"So they don't want to do any surgery because it's too dangerous. And the cancer is still growing inside me." I can feel the frustration radiating from him, combined with sadness and despair.

"I'm just so tired of it all, you know?" Tears glisten in his eyes, though he gives me a brave grin.

I close my eyes and see a cartoon image of my parents, buckled into that roller coaster car, skidding down, down, down the tracks to the lowest point of the ride.

Dear Father God, please, is there anything else that can be done? What is next?

"It's just getting harder and harder for your mother," he says. "I'm worried about her; she's tired of this, too."

I hold his hand tightly, fighting the urge to be a cheerleader and fill the air with false hopes. The truth is things look really bad. And I have absolutely no answers.

Later that afternoon Mom comes back to the hospital, showered and wearing a pretty blue sweater, coffee in hand. The kindly doctor who is overseeing Dad's local care in conjunction with the CTCA in Zion joins us and we sit down for a heart-to-heart conversation.

He brings up hospice care.

He talks about the risks of any future surgeries or treatments, and he is honest about their effectiveness. The eradication of all cancer in Dad's body is just not a real possibility.

Looking Dad right in the eye, he says, "People who choose to sign up for hospice care are ready to make the *quality* of the life they have remaining *better*, both for themselves and for their loved ones."

He then talks about how much better Dad will feel once all treatments are discontinued. Meds will only be administered to keep him pain-free and comfortable. He paints an appealing picture with terms like "comfort," "renewed energy," and "quality of life."

"You know," he grins, "I had one patient in hospice care who felt so good again he went out waterskiing!"

I have a brief, absurd thought that I myself am ready for hospice care ... and then I am flooded with such guilt for that thought that it overflows from my eyes, and I step away to the window. This is not about me.

As the doctor leaves the room and gives them time to talk, I look out the window over the sun-dappled, snowy grounds and blow my nose.

I hear Dad sigh heavily.

"Well, what do you think, Lyn? Is it time?"

I turn to see Mom and Dad quietly contemplating all that has been said. The pressing weight of the inevitable end enfolds them, yet I can see the desire for "home"–in so many variations of the word–in Dad's eyes. He is ready.

Mom takes his hand and nods her head, silently conceding.

At home I continue to grapple with my helplessness in all of this. Have my parents completely given up by calling in hospice care? Does it mean their–our–faith isn't strong? Is a miracle still possible at this late stage? I want to believe with all my heart that it is, but I just don't see it happening. Does this make me less of a believer? Does hospice care somehow weaken the chances of a miraculous healing taking place for Dad?

Today is Jim's birthday and we are planning to celebrate when he gets home from another business trip this evening. While Levi and Audrey help me wrap presents for him, I ponder what it really means to surrender. Is it the same as giving up? And I realize that, in a way, it is. It is the giving up of control, admitting I can do nothing in my own strength. That there are things–people, circumstances–that I have no power over.

I had surrendered my life to the Lord in college, acknowledging my need for Him. But that was just the first step. I had to surrender again during Courtney's health issues and the diagnosis of Williams Syndrome, letting go of my own desires for her life and what it would look like. I'm realizing the same will be true with each one of our children.

Later, Audrey and I sit on the floor of the family room and work on a puzzle together. I find myself thinking that, like the wooden shape in her chubby little fist, I am only holding one piece of the puzzle of the future. It is the Puzzle Designer alone who knows what the finished picture will look like.

I'm starting to see that surrendering is not just giving up control, it is relinquishing control *to* someone: the One who *does* have power over people and circumstances; the One Who, in *all* things, can bring good.

Though surrendering may feel like giving up, like I don't have faith, maybe it means I do.

The phone rings and I get up from the floor to answer it.

"Hey babe," says Jim. "I'm stuck in Atlanta; my flight home has been delayed."

"Oh, man...the kids will be so disappointed! I've got a Bill Knapp's chocolate cake waiting for you in the fridge."

"Well, in that case, I'll try extra hard to find another way to get home tonight," he laughs. "But we're probably gonna have to celebrate tomorrow. I'll keep you posted. Tell the kids good-night and I love them."

"Okay, hon, love you." I click off the phone, disappointed.

After I get the younger kids in bed for the night, Jared and I sit on the couch together and I quiz him with questions from the books he's been reading. The first round of The Battle of the Books is tomorrow night, and I have volunteered to be his team's coach. He's an avid reader, like his mom, and it's going to be a fun competition. He starts to head upstairs to go to bed, but then comes back to give me one last hug.

"I don't want Grandpa to die," he mumbles into my shoulder. "I don't have enough memories of him yet."

I hold him a little longer, a little closer.

I know, honey. I don't either.

Once he's upstairs, I settle in with my prayer journal.

As I finish penning my reflections and concerns, trying to put into words my struggle to surrender in this murky season of painful growth, I suddenly realize I'm hearing the garage door open. I look at the clock–it's almost 11 o'clock. Jim must have been able to find a flight home after all!

He opens the back door looking tired and bedraggled, but glad to be home. I give him a big birthday smooch and he asks, "Are the kids asleep?"

"Probably. But I'm sure they'd love to get up and celebrate with you while it's still your birthday."

We head up the stairs and gently wake up the kids. They're sleepy and confused at first, but when they see that Daddy is home and he says something about his birthday cake, they are soon running downstairs in their pajamas to the kitchen.

As we cut into the cake and scoop out vanilla ice cream, their faces glow with joy and love for Daddy, for ice cream, and for chocolate cake late at night. The light of the birthday candles is reassuring against the dark outside our windows. Knowing there is life, jubilant life, even in the shadow of death brings me great peace.

Chapter 10

But you, O Lord, are a shield about me,
my glory, and the lifter of my head.

Psalm 3:3 ESV

March 2006

Dad and I sit on the couch together in the walk-out basement of their condo. Outside it is cold but bright, and through the windows we can see the sunlight glistening on the still-frozen pond. Dad holds the instruction manual for an enormous remote-control sailboat that lays in pieces on the carpet in front of him.

Dad's friend Craig has joked in the past that you could hand Frankie a wooden pencil and, before your fingers release it, he would pull out the instruction manual and recite the entire thing to you. Dad has always been a hard-core information junkie.

Though his energy level seems to be stabilizing, today he lays the instructions aside after just a short time. It's too much for his brain at this point.

With an effort at cheer, he says to me, "Cheri, my dear, this spring I hope to put this bench out by the pond." He nods toward an old glider bench by the door that Jim has recently painted for him, adding "and sail this boat remotely. That's my short-term goal. It's good to have goals." Then his eyes fill and his voice breaks. "I don't have any more long-term goals."

I move closer to him and lay my head on his shoulder. There are no words I can say that will change or fix anything so I sit there, just loving him.

And hating this so much.

I think back to a Parker-Hannifin picnic for employees and their families that took place one summer when I was probably five years old. A picnic lunch was provided, there were games for us kids, and water balloons. I remember the hot sun and swinging on swings so high I could almost see over the treetops. And I recall getting off the swing set to see my dad walking toward me with his arms stretched out...and egg on his face.

Golden yolk covered one lens of his glasses and slimy egg white dripped onto his mustache and beard. He was laughing, but I burst into tears. I didn't understand what had happened. Who had done this to my dad?

He wiped his face and glasses with his ever-present, gross handkerchief and told me, grinning, that he had been in an egg toss, that it was a game, it was all in fun. I, however, was traumatized. The sight of my dad being disfigured this way, so unexpectedly, was very unsettling. Outside things weren't supposed to hurt him and I was very offended by the mere hint of attack, even with a raw egg.

These last several months have been one long, relentless attack on my dad. And at first I was extremely offended, indignant. Horrified. Like the little girl at the company picnic, afraid that an attack on my dad was somehow a direct threat to me; wanting to protect my dad but really wanting to protect myself.

Watching the one who had always been my safe place, my source of both guidance and encouragement, becoming so frail and so sad is excruciating. There is no question about Dad's salvation, and I know he does not fear death. It's this slow process of dying that's breaking our hearts.

I have never felt more powerless than I do in this moment.

I think of Dad's unconditional love poured out to me when I was questioning whether I would pursue a teaching career. It seems so long ago, such a minor question compared to what is happening right now. He had such grace for me even though he had no idea what the future held. He had entrusted me into God's hands, and I need to do the same for him now. I am learning that he is safer there, in God's will, than in my own. God's care is bigger than external forces, whether they be a raw egg or terminal cancer.

Later, Bruce comes over at Mom's request to sit with Dad and help him work on the boat.

Bruce Meles was working behind the counter at Bob's Hardware store in downtown Otsego when we first moved there. My Uncle Jerry, whose family had already been living in Otsego, recommended the store for its location and small-town care. It quickly became Dad's Saturday morning habit, whether he needed something from the hardware store or not.

He and Bruce struck up an easy friendship. Knowing my uncle and aunt and their family and hearing my cousins call him Uncle Frank soon led to Bruce and the other employees calling him "Uncle Frank" too. Bruce and his father were both sailors so when Dad discovered sailing, Bruce became his main man for all things nautical. They took a few trips together, Dad enjoying not just the beauty and peace of the water and the easy camaraderie, but learning the logistics, the technicalities, the terminology of sailing. Dad didn't just love learning, he lived to learn.

Reminiscing with Bruce today about previous sailing trips seems to ignite something in him. While they putter with the pieces, Dad turns to Bruce and says impulsively, "Let's charter a boat in Florida and go sailing."

Bruce looks up from the plastic parts in his hand at my dad–bald, shrunken, and leaning on a walker–and says, "Sure..." like a parent mollifying a child at bedtime with promises of marshmallows for breakfast.

Before the word is out of his mouth, Dad has wheeled himself across the room to the computer in the basement office. He has already pulled up the website for a 32-foot catamaran available for rent in Fort Lauderdale by the time Bruce looks over his shoulder. Dad picks up the phone and taps furiously, clumsily, with one finger on the keyboard. Bruce is stunned. *Leave it to Uncle Frank!*

Within days, Bruce is boning up on Florida Keys charts and colostomy care and is preparing for what Dad is calling "The Adventure of a Lifetime!"

The following week Simeon and Victoria come to visit. While living in New York City after grad school, Simeon discovered a passion for opera performance–and a pretty girl from Germany named Victoria. In 2004 they moved to Bielefeld, Germany, where Simeon performed at the local theater. The news that Dad has moved into hospice care in February leads Sim to do what he had been planning to do come summer: propose. Victoria says yes and they decide to make a trip to the U.S. to spend time with my parents and announce their engagement to the family.

Dad is thrilled–we all are. He has a soft spot for this lovely young woman with her musical accent and kind heart. And he doesn't waste any time putting Victoria to work. Victoria gets on the phone and makes the calls and flight reservations for the big trip, typing up itineraries at the direction of Captain Frank. Dad is in his element with someone to boss around, a plan to put into place, and the thought of being on the water once again.

On March 25, Mom drives him to the airport where he will meet up with Bruce and Craig. In Fort Lauderdale the guys are joined by John, who is already in Florida visiting family, and Uncle Mike, Dad's youngest brother, who lives there. These five men make up a genial motley crew, and Dad receives the utmost tenderness from the other four as they heave him onboard and seat him at the helm of this seaworthy vessel.

This "Adventure of a Lifetime" is the ultimate Dad thing –organizing something exciting not just for his own enjoyment but to draw people together, to share the adventure with people he cares for. His detailed preparations, his determination to create a memorable experience for his friends, and many prayers lifted by everyone else at home result in a flawless excursion. Underneath bright blue skies and propelled by prevailing winds, the five men, brothers in Christ and brothers in spirit, spend three days soaking up the beauty around them and the friendship between them.

A year later, three of these men would write detailed recollections of this trip for my mom, a gift of memory that allowed her to enjoy the trip with Frankie from a distance. They would write fondly of Dad's attention to detail, even with his tumorous brain, that made everything come together in perfect form. They would remember not a single complaint coming from his mouth; rather, that the joy *they* experienced on the trip became *his* joy.

In the letters, they write about how Dad suggested he clear a space for them at the airport bar by opening his colostomy bag; how he had fallen asleep on the "trampoline" at the front of the boat until an enormous wave caught him from underneath. How the five of them had laughed into the night over wine and cards, and Dad and Mike's tender moments of brotherly love, saying the last things that needed to be said.

At the end of his letter, Bruce painted a vivid picture that captured the essence of Dad on that trip. When a pod of dolphins decided to swim between the hulls of the catamaran one afternoon, Dad struggled to see them from his seat at the tail of the boat. Grabbing onto the winch handle with a shaky hand and peering over the top of the cabin, he lifted his face to get a better view of this spectacular show of beauty in the glistening sunshine. At that moment Bruce caught a glimpse of Dad's face under the wind-blown brim of his Tilley hat, looking like the captain of everything, his face a palette of every emotion, of pleasure and pain, of sadness, of joy.

Mom would tell me several months later that as Craig pushed Dad in his wheelchair toward her in the airport, she felt a brief surge of hope that there might be another trip for her and her husband in the future. But when she and Dad locked eyes and she saw a tear make its way down his tired, sun-tanned cheek, she knew that this would be his last trip on this earth.

Chapter 11

–to comfort all who mourn,
and provide for those who grieve in Zion –
to bestow on them a crown of beauty instead of ashes,
the oil of joy instead of mourning,
and a garment of praise instead of a spirit of despair.

Isaiah 61:3 NIV

April 2006

"Alright girls, are you ready for bed?" I enter my daughters' shared bedroom and turn off the light. A bejeweled nightlight shines in the corner of the room as they snuggle down in their beds underneath matching pink comforters. I lie down next to Audrey, who cuddles up close.

"Who wants to pray?" I ask, stroking her cheek and closing my eyes. I'm exhausted as usual by this time of night. I've already tucked Levi in and Jared is downstairs, staying up a little later with Jim to work on the model train set in the basement.

"I know!" Courtney says with a huge smile, popping back up in bed. "Let's sing instead!"

A hidden blessing amid Courtney's challenges is that music seems to be the great healer. People with Williams Syndrome tend to have an intimate relationship with music, a connection to it like no other. Music has soothed many an anxious moment for Court, a flowing comfort that fills in all the gaps.

And music seems appropriate right now, when I feel like I am running out of words to pray on behalf of my father. There is a weight of sadness underlying everything –consuming worry for my parents, Jim's travel and work schedule, the busyness of the kids, and church activities that I continue to keep my mind distracted from grief.

"That's a good idea," I say softly. "Lay back down, honey, and we'll sing."

"Father, I adore you ... Lay my life before you ... How I love you ..." I begin. Courtney harmonizes instinctively from her twin bed.

Audrey rests her cheek on her chubby arm and sucks on her tongue next to me. She doesn't always sing, but I pray the words and melodies will seep into her little soul. I thank God for the gift of song for so many reasons.

I can almost hear the Holy Spirit interceding for me with groanings too deep for words.

Easter is drawing near with the heart-wrenching knowledge that Dad may not live to see it. I have taken the girls shopping for Easter dresses, knowing deep down these pastel fabrics that twirl when they spin will soon be funeral attire. I have bought myself a new outfit for Easter, too, but shopping brings no joy.

My belief in the resurrection of Jesus–and knowing that Dad believes the same–is the anchor for my soul this Easter, and with fists practically clenched I am determined to celebrate it no matter how much it hurts.

I find myself waking up in the middle of the nights now, thinking about my mom. What would I be doing if I knew my husband would soon be gone from me? I can hardly breathe at this thought, this enormous weight of grief I feel for my mother. I curl up against Jim's warm, strong body and I can't imagine his side of the bed being empty forever. I mentally put myself in Mom's position. If it were me, I'd be climbing right up on the hospital bed with my husband, absorbing every morsel of warmth, smell, skin, breath. Hanging on for dear life.

I was helpless as I watched my parents' journey through cancer unfold. There was nothing I could do, no judgment I could make, no explanation I could give. This was out of my hands. What is it about death that is so consuming, so fearful, so inexplicable? Is it that death is the great equalizer, a physical battle we can fight but ultimately cannot win?

Though our lives are lived uniquely, in the reality of death we are all the same. Grief is an ocean in which every single one of us will eventually find ourselves; the place where we are stripped clean of any pretense of control, any false assumption that we "can fix this." Is this what is meant by "the fellowship of suffering"?

Recently Mom told me that while she pushed Dad in his wheelchair around the winding roads of the condo complex, they talked about his funeral. He told her what songs he wanted sung: "Peace in the Valley" and "I'll Fly Away." He said he didn't want paper plates and Jell-O; he wanted everyone to enjoy a home cooked meal on real dinner plates –comfort food. He told her he wanted it to be a celebration. "I'll be home," he said.

The day before Easter Sunday we all gather at a park near Mom and Dad's condo. Uncle Jerry and Aunt Judy are there, and most of my siblings and their kids. Simeon is still in town and Pete and Reneé are here until Monday. A few friends of my parents' stop by as well. The weather is sunny and mild; we hide eggs and do crafts with the kids at the pavilion, taking turns to drive up to the house and sit with Dad.

When it's my turn, I bring Courtney and Audrey with me. Dad lies in the sunroom on his hospital bed, sunlight warming the room as Alan Jackson sings hymns from a CD player nearby. Dad isn't speaking much these days, but he smiles at the girls as they take turns sitting up on the bed with him. Audrey gently bounces her stuffed dog Sandy over Dad's frail limbs, onto the limp shoulders that once held me up as I towered over the deep end of the campground pool.

I fight the urge to throw myself next to him on the bed and weep, to beg him not to go. Instead, I find myself chattering stupidly and fussing over the girls.

As we prepare to leave, I lift my wiggling toddler from the bed and tell Dad again how much I love him. He stares at me intently, tracking me with wide eyes, trying to convey words to me. I notice this, and take his weak hand in mine, swallowing the lump in my throat.

"I know, Dad. You love me too."

With all his energy he musters a nod and a whisper: "Very... much."

These are the last words he will ever speak to me.

I am not gifted with a beautiful singing voice–that talent went to my younger siblings. However, for this one season I sing in our church choir. The following day, Easter Sunday, I put on a garment of praise in this spirit of heaviness, lifting my voice in worship that unties the knots of grief in my throat.

Through worship I see that it truly is possible to be happy and heartbroken at the same time, to feel joy and pain intertwined so tightly my heart will surely burst.

My safety net, the unconditional love, support, and security given to me by my parents, is being torn asunder with the impending death of my father.

But I have a deeper, stronger, hope.

When Simeon calls me Tuesday morning with the news that Dad is gone, I race up to Zeeland going 80 miles an hour. Even at that speed the drive takes an hour, and my thoughts wander.

I was a little girl, maybe in first grade, when Dad got us a puppy for Christmas. My parents weren't ever animal people but wanted to try a family pet. Snoopy, a mutt, grew fast and large and was soon jumping on everyone; he was more work and more chaos than our young family could handle. It wasn't long before Dad decided it would be better to give him away to a family who would love and take care of him.

"But Dad," I said mournfully, as we stood in the kitchen. "Why? Why does he have to go?"

"Ah ... Cheri ..." Dad sighed as he swiped his hand through the hair over his forehead. He sat down on a chair by the table and pulled me into his lap. "It was a hard decision. I've had a lot of mixty motions."

As a six-year-old, I could understand that description, that feeling of "mixty." I could hold my hand out and wobble it back and forth and know that described how I was feeling.

"But," he continued, "sometimes we have to do what we don't want to do ... because it's just better that way."

I wouldn't learn until much later the phrase "mixed emotions," but Dad helped me understand that sometimes you must endure what is difficult–even if it hurts or makes you feel sad–for a greater good, a better purpose. And you can have both good and bad feelings about it.

I have such mixty motions today. Part of me feels relieved that this long, difficult road has finally ended. And part of me will just really miss my dad.

◇ ◇ ◇

1993

After our wedding, Jim and I had moved to Michigan's Upper Peninsula. It was a good first year for us in that we were forced to rely on one another, to work through things together. It was a blessing in disguise that cell phones, texting, and email (though in the works) were not available to us yet, and long-distance phone calls were too expensive. We had to learn to talk things through with each other.

But I was extremely homesick. We visited a few churches together a handful of times, but our under-developed faith and lack of discipline led to more Sundays sleeping in than getting up for church. As a result, we never got plugged into a church family and had very few friends. I missed my family, especially Reneé and the chubby, kissable cheeks of my nephew. I missed my parents and the chaotic but familiar Esper family dinner table. I couldn't wait for our trips home, even though it meant nine hours in the car and scraping up enough change to pay the $1.50 toll to cross the Mackinac Bridge.

One day in late November while I was student teaching, my class of second graders was in the gymnasium practicing songs for their upcoming Christmas concert. The theme for this year was music from around the country and around the world. As I sat in the gym and listened contentedly, the opening guitar music of "Rocky Mountain High" by John Denver suddenly began to play over the cassette player.

My heart, aching already with homesickness and the adjustments of new marriage, reacted with such intensity that I had to climb down quickly from the bleachers. Sobbing in a stall in the girls' bathroom, I wanted more than anything to be back in the green van with my dad at the wheel and Mom by his side, on a camping trip one more time, looking out the window with not a care in the world. I missed my parents, I missed being a little girl, and I didn't like not knowing what the future held for me.

In college I had pursued a degree in elementary education because I knew that I wanted a family and children someday, and if that didn't happen right away it seemed being a teacher would be the next best thing. Growing up in a large family had given me plenty of experience with kids, so it seemed to make sense.

But I was beginning to realize that my heart's desire was to be like my mom. I wanted the life my mom had. I knew it wasn't always easy but in my eyes it was honorable, steady, it provided a foundation and a sense of steadfastness to those around her.

She was organized and reliable; she always used her creativity and talents to help people. She was generous and freely gave to others from her place of security, provided for and supported by my dad. I too wanted to stay at home and raise a family; I wanted to have babies with Jim and pour our love into them. I wanted to be generous, productive; to provide a haven of stability for those I loved. To me that was a worthy goal. While I thought teaching was the closest thing to parenting I could do and get paid for, I really wanted to allow the good that had filled my childhood to overflow into my own family.

After my graduation that December from CMU, a two-week-long visit with our families over Christmas helped ease some of the homesickness. We enjoyed the Esper family tradition of Mom's marinated steaks on the grill on Christmas Eve and opened presents on the blue carpet of the living room. I shopped with my mom and my sister, and Jim and I celebrated Christmas with his side of the family, too. We then made the long drive back up to our tiny apartment in Negaunee, where a letter from Dad was already waiting in our mailbox.

January 9, 1993

Hi kids,

Not much to say after our time together.

The extra $50 is our gift of celebration. Don't be shy if you need more–I've never seen a better investment than you two.

Isn't God great?

Keep praying and be patient – 'fore you know it you'll be ol' and gray like us.

See you soon,

Love, Dad

I worked as a substitute teacher for the rest of that school year, but I felt at loose ends and unsure of myself. I felt incredibly guilty for taking five and a half years of college to conclude that I wasn't sure I wanted to teach!

That spring I poured out my heart in a letter home; Dad quickly responded.

March 13, 1993

Dear Cheri,

We received your nice letter yesterday. Whew–where does a father start?

Today is Saturday and I'm waiting for dinner to finish cooking. I'm listening to MY radio program (Bluegrass, you know).

We miss you too, Cher, in a very special way. We are so happy for you, plus you're such a special friend now that you're "mature" and married (especially to such a nice fellow.) So, it's a bitter-sweet kind of missing without any bitter!

I still miss my mom and dad occasionally in a very special way–I believe it's the process of life (on earth anyway), of birth-life-death.

Isn't it wonderful that we have such fond, great loving memories that we just still want to be together? Our lives are still quite involved together–more than just acquaintances. So, thank God for the love we have for each other when you get a little home-lonesome.

I have ALWAYS said what a good thing it was that Mom and I lived away for a few years to establish OUR life on its own. I am quite domineering, so I think it's great you guys are doing so well. Jim is an absolute Peach of a Pick. I have 100% confidence that things will work out for you (The Balcoms) here in Michigan or wherever you land. Home is where your heart is (NOT your hat–that's the house).

And another thing. A college education is a wonderful

thing–I tell my students it's a key that unlocks many doors. I trust you and I really want your happiness. I don't care if you teach in a school system or exactly what you do. Use your wonderful personality, your skills, your knowledge, your gifts from God to help other people–and maybe make a few bucks. Believe me, you have what it takes to succeed. Period. Pray and follow God's lead–I'm on your side. It doesn't have to be teaching and it doesn't have to be now.

I do love you both, I don't want you to be worried about what I think–I'm proud of you–of course I'll take full credit for you being such a neat, wonderful person. Had you turned out a bum, it would be your fault. Ha Ha

If you don't understand my rambling–I LOVE YOU.

Love, Dad

When I was a child, it was easy for me to believe that God loved me unconditionally because I had received that kind of love from Mom and Dad.

I realize now that *He* was where Mom and Dad learned to love that way, that *He* was the well they drew from. Their knowledge of Him and relationship with Him in Christ informed their care for me and our family. *He* is my true "safety net."

Before Dad's illness, I felt I had reached a point where everything seemed to fall into place: husband, children, home, church, a blossoming relationship with my parents and siblings. But these were not guarantees of anything.

Everything else–everyone else–is frail, temporary, flawed. Every one of us longs for sure footing beneath us; something in our lives that gives us a sense of grounding, of safety, of strength to hold us. God had to show me–through pain–that even though He had blessed me with wonderful people and circumstances in my life that provided stability, *He* is the ultimate security.

He told us that trouble would come, that there would be pain and hardship and loss.

But He also said, "Never will I leave you; never will I forsake you." (Hebrews 13:5 NIV)

In the sunroom at the condo, after I place a last, gentle kiss on Dad's cold forehead, my siblings, my mom, and I join hands and Mom says a final prayer. I realize that the sadness I am feeling now is not so much a desire for Dad to stay here on earth with us. I believe that Dad is without pain now and in the presence of the Lord for eternity, and I'm so glad.

I just wish I could be there with him.

It's bittersweet, without the bitter.

CHAPTER 12

For I am the LORD your God who takes
hold of your right hand and says to you,
Do not fear; I will help you.

Isaiah 41:13 NIV

2001-2002

A miscarriage right around Courtney's second birthday had shaken me. Though the pregnancy was unexpected, we had embraced the idea of adding a third child to our family with excitement. But after the loss, the grieving, and the D&C, I couldn't help but wonder if there was now something wrong with my body. I had birthed a child with physical and mental challenges and then I had a miscarriage? What was going on? During this time, I clung to Psalm 37:4: "Delight yourself in the Lord, and He will give you the desires of your heart." (NIV)

Just a couple of months after my Dad's heartfelt Thanksgiving Day prayer in 1999, not long after the miscarriage, we discovered we were pregnant once again. Dad's prayer had been for the families we were becoming: the Espers, the Balcoms, the Yakes, and more to come. When an early ultrasound showed that all was well, we emailed the pictures to our family, jokingly referring to the little bean inside me as "Mordecome." After a brief but intense labor, Levi James was born calmly sucking his two fingers, an exact replica of his father (except for the finger-sucking part).

Life became busier, more fun, and more cramped in our tiny house, so just before Levi was a year old we bought a house in a small town south of Kalamazoo. It was a two-story Cape Cod in a quiet, tree-lined neighborhood. As we swam with the kids in the inground pool the night after moving in, Jim and I looked at each other in disbelief: we *never* thought we could own a house so nice. God had graciously provided the desires of my heart, and then some! I was overwhelmed with gratitude.

One evening in the kitchen not long after moving in, I opened the oven to pull out the casserole I was making for dinner. Though battling a cold, I attempted to breathe in the comforting smell of stuffing and cream of mushroom soup bubbling atop four juicy chicken breasts.

Out of the corner of my eye I noticed 13-month-old Levi crawling along the kitchen floor behind me.

"Watch out, baby," I sing-songed. "HOT!"

I opened the oven door only partially to prevent him from reaching out for the hot oven, while I stuck my mitted hand in carefully to remove the casserole dish. But I couldn't prevent the door from snapping back up and catching the underside of my forearm with a sharp smack and a hiss.

"Ouch!" I exclaimed, practically throwing the casserole onto the stovetop. Though I was so thankful that it was me and not Levi, that scalding hurt like a son of a gun. As I stuck my arm underneath the cold running water in the sink, I tried not to cry.

Jim picked up Levi and walked over to the sink. "You okay?"

I could see the burn already beginning to blister, red and ugly. My head throbbed.

"I don't feeeel gooood..." I whined, sniffling.

"Why don't you try to get into the doctor's office tomorrow to get that looked at? Maybe he can give you something for your cold, too."

I made the appointment and Jim met me in the parking lot a few minutes beforehand. We had learned from previous appointments that it was easier, if he was available, for him to sit with the kids in the van while I went inside–less chaos in the waiting room. I came outside afterwards and walked right up to the driver's side window. Jim rolled it down.

"Well? What did he say?"

I looked him in the eye and said with a slowly rising hysteria, "I'm pregnant."

His shock quickly turned into laughter; mine into tears. Don't get me wrong, I was happy! But I was overwhelmed.

I kept this news from my extended family for a little while, mostly to make sure I wasn't going to wake up and realize it had all been a weird, hormonal dream. Although

Jim and I had talked about having four children, casually thinking that would be a good number to shoot for, number three wasn't even walking yet. In fact, I had just stopped nursing him a month earlier. I had finally gotten back into my regular jeans, and the thought of pulling out the box of maternity clothes, not to mention going through labor and delivery again, was staggering.

At the time, Reneé and Pete had just announced that they were expecting their first child and I didn't want to take away from this exciting news. My sister Miriam was planning a wedding for the following July and, if my calculations were correct, this little surprise would be six weeks old by then. I would be a breastfeeding bridesmaid.

It was a lot to take in. But I tried to swallow the rising panic in my chest and thank God for this gift of new life. This is what I had wanted, right?

What do you do when God gives you everything you've asked for? I had written the script for the life I desired when I was a newlywed with a fresh diamond ring on my finger: marriage, staying home to raise our kids like my mother did, a house at some point. Casseroles. Church. A minivan.

The more God allowed my life to become full of the things I desired, the more I found myself scrabbling to control them. I had embraced my role as wife and stay-at-home mom with gusto, proudly absorbing every moment of pregnant backaches, dirty diapers, lullabies, housecleaning, grocery shopping, doctors' appointments, date nights, dinner guests, prayers, Bible lessons, and laundry. Though sometimes I complained, usually with humor among fellow moms, deep down I loved every single second of it. The domestic life was made for me and I for it.

I won't lie; there's a certain level of confidence that comes with each child you birth and manage to raise for a few years without harming. Even Courtney's diagnosis and challenges were still currently within my realm of control, for the most part. I had indeed reached my goal of becoming my mother. Loving husband: check. Precious children: check. Comfortable house: check. Community to serve: check. Everything was lining up.

But by my thirties, something inside me had begun to coil and tighten like a spring–a desire to not only become like my mom and recreate my childhood, but to do an even better job of it than my parents did. I took their somewhat casual approach to church and raised it to taking my kids to Sunday School and church every single Sunday. I jumped on the homeschool bandwagon of the 1990s, convincing myself it would guarantee Christian kids who would finish school with better Bible knowledge than I had achieved by age 35. Maybe it would even produce a missionary!

What my dad had once referred to as "Churchianity," what he considered all the extra doings of the church that people got caught up in apart from sharing the gospel, and something that had turned him off from organized religion for a spell, I now embraced with vigor. I viewed it as just an outpouring of love and gratitude for my salvation.

I knew that I could not earn God's grace and didn't deserve it, but couldn't I at least pay it back? Wasn't God worthy of that?

The looser, gentler Christianity of my Jesus-hippie parents, which I still acknowledged as a huge influence on me, began to fade away as I found myself striving for a more perfect devotion. Not only was I thriving in my role of "Domestic Engineer," I was attempting to become the "Spiritual Engineer" too.

I took very seriously the responsibility of training up children in the Lord, of always guiding their steps in His direction. This is a worthy intention, and even now I believe it is important. But I had expectations, of my husband and myself, and they were high. When expectations and outcomes became my main focus, I was often disappointed. All I began to see was where others, and myself, constantly fell short. The sphere of "righteousness" in which I had enveloped myself tightened like a noose around my poor family–and my own heart.

"I had uh accident, Mommy!"

I may or may not have sworn in the middle of praying. But this was the second potty accident Courtney had had that day, hence the uninvited swear word.

I leaned over my end-of-second trimester belly and placed Levi, now 17 months old, on the floor. He began to whimper, disappointed that our special cuddle time before his nap had been interrupted.

This semi-quiet time in the rocking chair with Levi was finally the chance I needed to talk to God a little bit after having had an ugly hormonal cry in the shower that morning. We needed to touch base. I needed to reach out to Him even if we didn't touch. I was overwhelmed.

To the background noise of Jared, an energetic six-year-old, and Courtney, now four, I tried to take a minute while rocking Levi to offer up a plea for help, strength, and mercy.

Jim was traveling again this week for work and wouldn't be home for another couple of days. Levi, though almost a year and a half, was still not walking. I didn't know how much longer I could carry him and my pregnant belly up and down the stairs! I was six months pregnant and trying to picture today's scenario with a nursing newborn added to the mix. And then came Courtney's announcement. *Will she ever be completely potty-trained?*

She tip-toed into Levi's room, spread-legged and dripping. I heaved myself up out of the rocking chair, took her hand, and scootched her around the corner to the bathroom. As I put a clean pair of Dora the Explorer underpants on her wiggly little body, I could hear Jared entertaining Levi with his toys in the other room, crashing Hot Wheels cars together to make him laugh.

Through my exhaustion, I couldn't help but smile. I had such a good life; I had the life that I had always hoped for, with a few minor unexpected turns.

Why did I feel the way I did that day? Was I just a tired, pregnant mom filled with extra hormones? Or was it something deeper? I thought about a recurring dream that had been showing up as I slept. I would be driving my minivan fast with all the kids in the back. Suddenly, something would appear in front of me–a cliff, a mangled bridge over a canyon, another car–and I would slam on the brakes. But no matter how hard I stomped on them, even if I stood on them, in my dream I could never get my van to slow down.

We arrived home from the hospital on a sunny Sunday in June to see a pink sign on the lawn and bobbing balloons above it–our kind neighbors celebrating with us the birth of our new daughter. As I carefully climbed out of the van, Jim set the car seat down on the driveway so the kids could meet their new sister. They ran over to see her and Jim's mom, who had been staying with the kids, walked up with a broad smile. I noticed that she had helped them plant pink and white begonias all along the front sidewalk. God bless her.

"Well, what do you think?" Jim said to the family as they crowded around the car seat.

"Yep. It's a baby!" declared Jared. "Can I see her extension cord?"

"You mean umbilical cord, you goof," said Jim, playfully punching Jared's shoulder. Jared dramatically fell onto the grass, grabbing Jim's leg as he fell; the two started to wrestle.

"Oooooooooh, why hello there, you darling thing!" Courtney exclaimed. She immediately presented her whole face in the car seat, crooning and making baby talk. Meanwhile Levi, busy slurping on a popsicle that dripped in purple rivulets down his arm, wordlessly crouched down to inspect.

He had *finally* taken his first steps a few months earlier and was now walking with confidence. He thrust his popsicle toward Baby Audrey's face and vocalized something that ended in a question mark, clearly asking if she'd like a bite. This was such a tender moment, but all I could see was that grape popsicle ready to drip onto Audrey's crisp, white receiving blanket. I quickly pulled the car seat away from Levi's sloppy but generous offer.

On my last visit to the midwife a few days earlier, she had performed a natural little procedure designed to encourage contractions to start. That evening, as I felt twinges in my belly, I decided to take a brisk walk around the neighborhood to keep them going in the hopes it would turn into actual labor.

"Hey Mom!" Jared had hollered from our driveway as I headed home. "Did you have any more contraptions?"

I laughed, gently corrected him, and pulled off my sweaty socks and shoes.

"Come walk out back with me," I said, taking his hand. We walked barefoot around the backyard as the sun set and the night grew cool, happily discussing how it would soon be warm enough to swim in our pool.

Later that night, in full blown labor as Jim drove me to the hospital, I suddenly realized I had never made time to shave my legs and paint my toenails like I had towards the end of my other pregnancies. As I slid into the stirrups on the delivery table, I saw with horror that the bottoms of my feet were cracked and dirty from walking barefoot outside.

Around 4 a.m. little Audrey Leigh arrived in all her round-cheeked, unexpected glory, a poignant reminder that I just can't control everything.

2006

On a blustery day in May we gather at the marina in Holland, on the shore of Lake Michigan, to release Dad's ashes. Four of my siblings and myself, my mom, my parents' dear friends Craig and John, and Bruce from the Hardware store, meet up with a friend who has offered to take us out on his gorgeous sailboat for the day. It is cold and windy, but the sun is shining.

Dad had requested his ashes be released ten miles out from the shore onto the water he loves; but Mom puts her foot down this time and says five miles out will be enough. She doesn't want to get too far from the sight of land because the waves are quite choppy.

The fact that my parents ever sailed together, let alone owned a sailboat, is a beautiful mystery to me. My mother never learned to swim. She had shared with me, just once, a casual comment about a swimming lesson she'd had as a child–she'd been thrown into the water and expected to figure it out. The fact that she was ever willing to climb aboard a sailboat and ride out into the wind with her husband is both astonishing and adorable–Mom in her inflatable suspenders, one hand holding a glass of wine and the other clinging tightly to the railing.

Today we chat pleasantly and make jokes as we motor out, and then our voices raise with the sails as the brisk wind picks up. It is cold but exhilarating. My dad had such respect for the wind, a passion for the water, and a love of being in motion upon it. We channel these memories of him as we laugh and take turns at the helm. Despite our jovial banter, emotion is strung tightly along the lines of the sailboat. I sit between Kelly and Reneé in layers of jackets and a headband over my ears, feeling somber through my smile.

Mom's face betrays her pain as the boat slows at our pausing point. All conversation dwindles as Simeon opens the box and pulls out the bag of ashes. It is surreal that this is all that's left of my father's body; the reality of the words "from dust to dust" hits me hard. As Craig says a brief prayer, in my heart I praise God for Dad's physical body, his physical life that affected my life–my soul–so much. And I praise Him for the life that is promised when the dust has blown away, the life Dad is already enjoying.

This is the final act of letting go.

I look over at Mom, who sits on the cushions under the hull and out of the wind. She has never been on a sailboat without Dad. Simeon told me that Mom spent the last nights of Dad's life lying next to him on his hospital bed, absorbing every last morsel of warmth, smell, skin, breath. Hanging on for dear life.

Her face now is drawn, her eyes red. I can only imagine the metaphors going through her head; she is a boat without a rudder, a ship without an anchor, a sail without wind to fill it.

I think back to a day not long ago when I had lamented to my mom over lunch about how hard it was sometimes, the running of the household and caring for four young children while Jim was traveling for work. He is such a hands-on dad that it is so noticeable when he is gone; something that I took for granted until he was not there.

"Oh Cher. I know how you feel," she said. "I remember one time in the little house in Kalamazoo; it was during the blizzard of '78. Your dad was in Chicago for something, I don't even remember what. But he was stuck there because of the weather, and I didn't know when he would be coming home. The schools were all closed, we had a foster baby, and I was watching a couple of neighbor kids because their mother had to work ... and I was just so overwhelmed and tired."

"I went into the bathroom, closed the door, and sat on the edge of the bathtub. I tried to pray but just felt too weak. And then ... I had the strongest sense of the Lord saying, 'Reach up, Lynda. Hold on to my hand.' And, as silly as it sounds, that's what I did." She had chuckled, remembering. "I lifted my hand right there and pictured myself just grabbing onto his strong hand. And he carried me through."

I pray she will reach up her hand and grab onto God's now.

With a soft whoosh, the wind carries Dad's ashes over the waters of Lake Michigan to a safe, eternal harbor.

◇ ◇ ◇

Four and a half years earlier, on September 11, 2001, I had to force myself to walk away from the TV in the family room. The relentless coverage of the smoking–and then collapsing–World Trade Center towers would be forever seared into my brain. As I stepped out of the sliding door into our backyard, I stood with my hands on my hips looking into the clean blue sky and breathing in the fresh, pure air. It was a gorgeous, peaceful day. The sunshine glistened on the surface of our swimming pool as I leaned on the wooden fence. Though the usual airplanes flying overhead to and from the Kalamazoo airport had already been stilled, I could hear birds chirping and the sound of a neighbor mowing the yard. A garbage truck grunted in between houses a few streets over.

In spite of the lovely day, my heart was heavy with sadness and I was filled with a profound sense of guilt. How could it be possible that I was allowed to walk into my peaceful backyard this morning and stand in the sunshine to the tune of my neighbor's lawnmower, while hundreds of horrified people were combing the dusty streets of New York City clutching photos of their loved ones, searching and calling for them among the chaos and the rubble? How could this be? How could life, my life, be allowed to go on so unencumbered in the wake of such tragedy?

These were my feelings, my questions, yet again after the passing of my father. The irony was unsettling as I took pictures of my three-year-old before her first ballet recital just a few days after Dad's memorial service. Her blonde hair was pulled tightly into a bun and her chubby cheeks split into a grin against the backdrop of leftover funeral flowers that filled my living room. Orchids, chrysanthemums, tulips in every hue; white-ribboned peace lilies and baskets of ferns filled my house with glorious color, but with the reminder that death had been a recent visitor.

How dare I smile and applaud my miniature ballerina on stage while I sat next to my mother, the incalculable weight of grief etched into her puffy eyes and her brave smile? I grieved for my little ballerina in blue feathers who would carry no memory of her grandpa. Her ears would never hear him call her "Al," the affectionate nickname he had given her at birth by lumping her initials together.

How can the joy of life and the grief of death be allowed to co-exist like this? I felt like I was swimming underwater along a brilliant coral reef, my lungs bursting in pain with the need for air but unable to pull myself away from the sheer beauty of life in front of me.

Acknowledging that my grief was different than my mother's grief created another realm of guilt. Yes, this was breaking my heart, but my home was still full of life and distraction; though I mourned and missed my dad terribly, I still got into bed at night with my warm husband. While I could share my grief with my siblings on the phone, Mom was rattling around in her big, beautiful condo and sleeping alone.

Not only was she a widow at just 59, she was alone in a fairly new home and city. She still kept in touch with a few close friends from Otsego, but the cocoon of grief and sadness sequestered her for a long time. We kids could only do so much, being physically spread out and away from her and busy with young children.

We called and checked in, not always knowing what to say but learning quickly not to call after dark. Those were her hardest hours; the hours when she and Dad should've been enjoying a glass of wine together, some cheese and crackers, maybe some music, maybe a game of Scrabble. The pain was too concrete then, the night too hollow. We learned to hold plans loosely, as she was apt to change her mind depending on the day and how she was feeling. What else could we do?

Whether I wanted to or not, I found myself setting expectations for her grief that clearly came from my non-experience of losing my spouse. I felt an impatience that flowed from my helplessness; I just wanted things to go back to the way they were, though I knew they never could.

One day as I was reading a novel by Elizabeth Berg called *Home Safe*, I came across a passage that jarred me. The main character, who had just lost her husband, relays these thoughts during lunch with a friend:

> *"Midge was not experiencing grief. When you were, you did not remark upon it and then sip your iced tea. If you spoke about your pain in any truthful way, you clenched your fists in your lap. You looked out the window to find something to distract you, to stop a flow of thoughts that would quickly overwhelm you. Or you laughed that thin laugh that is not laughter at all but tears, rerouted."*

I paused, re-read the paragraph, then sighed. Tears, rerouted. My poor mom. Why was I expecting her to reroute for me? Why couldn't I have more grace for her?

It was almost obscene the way life kept moving forward. Just a week after Dad's memorial service, my busy family got a puppy, which of course is a wise decision when you have four kids under the age of 11 and you are in the middle of grieving. (Turns out, it was pretty wise.)

That fall we purchased a used motorhome as an act of intentionality about continuing to camp with the kids–another way for me to keep the memory of my dad alive. My eyes filled with tears as I pictured walking my dad through the giant Class C motorhome, hearing him use one of his favorite phrases, "That is *slick*," as we showed him all the bells and whistles. I could hear him saying, "You know what you should do ...," could see him rubbing his hands together as he listed all the places we could take the kids. In the blink of a twinkling eye, he would have a huge family camping trip planned.

Later, while camping in the Upper Peninsula, I got a phone call from Miriam who announced they were pregnant with their second child. I was elated for her and Seth, but at the same time felt a deep sadness all over again. I grieved for my two youngest children and for Frank's grandkids yet to be born, because they would never remember or know their Grandpa Esper, never hear his belly laugh or see his "saucer eyes." Though they would often hear us repeat it, they would never hear his voice playfully chiding, "A card laid is a card played!" when we played Wizard. They would not sail with him on his boat, they would not ride with him on the lawnmower; they would not hear him sing "Happy birthday," painfully out of tune, adding his famous whistle at the end as the candles were extinguished.

Most of all they would not witness the daily, exuberant joy he spread to everyone he met, like a paintbrush filled with sunshine. They would not hear him talk about the grace of God saving him, a sinner, and see his eyes water as he spoke of "the veil torn in two," humbled all over again in the re-telling.

CHAPTER 13

Teach us to number our days,
that we may gain a heart of wisdom.

Psalm 90:12 NIV

2011

It's a sunny spring day, and today I feel cute. I am wearing a gauzy leopard print top with bell sleeves, jeans, and black boots with a chunky heel. My earrings and car keys jingle confidently as I climb into the Suburban for the short drive to the school.

When my husband and I were married in 1992, my hair was long and perm-curly; the "mall bangs" I wore in college toned down to a soft fringe for the wedding. After the wedding I experimented with different lengths through various stages of life: I went short while student-teaching so the kids would take me seriously, then grew it out long and straight while I worked at a bank until Jared was born. I chopped it close to my head while pregnant with Courtney hoping for a quicker morning routine, but ended up hating the look. By the time Levi came it was somewhere between short and long, kind of curly but needed help with a curling iron. My poor husband, who preferred the long curly hair of our college days, was long-suffering (pun intended) when it came to me and my locks.

I finally grew it back to the way he liked it in time for a romantic trip together to Aruba after Audrey turned two. But a year later, not long before Dad got sick and with four kids ages 3 to 10, I cut it short again. The latest style for moms was sassy, with longer side-swiped bangs tucked behind the ears, and the back all choppy.

It's funny how my hairstyle was really a message I was trying to convey–a picture of "This Is Who I Am." At the time I was in my element, a stay-at-home mom running a household, dating my husband while tag-team parenting; with one child in public school and homeschooling a couple of the younger ones; busy with Bible studies and serving at church. I felt like a boss running my little world–not without mistakes or mishaps–as efficiently as a well-oiled machine. And I needed a matching hairdo: efficient but cute, organized yet fun.

Today, though, my hair is finally starting to grow out from the last short "mom" haircut, and I'm liking it longer. I'm feeling really good.

I am also in a hurry. I live just two minutes away, yet I am late getting to the middle school where Jim is meeting me for Courtney's IEP. Levi and Audrey are going to walk over from the elementary building after school and wait in the hall until our meeting is over. As I race along in my Suburban, I suddenly notice the police car behind me flashing its red and blue lights. *Aargh!* This is a school zone and I am going way over the 25-mph speed limit.

Sigh. I pull over.

"License and registration please."

I am right outside the school windows. My poor kids would be so embarrassed if they saw me! What a great example I am for Jared, our newly licensed driver. I pray silently that I am not seen by anyone I know in the school building. *At least I look good today.*

Finally I am striding down the hall of the middle school to our meeting. Everything goes smoothly, and we sign the IEP for next year. Audrey and Levi don't fight too much while waiting out in the hall. Jim loads everybody up to run a couple errands afterward while I head back home to start dinner.

When I arrive there is a message on our answering machine from the hospital, asking me to call to schedule a recheck on my mammogram. I am 41 years old, and just a few days earlier I had gone in for what was only the second mammogram I've ever had. Surely this is nothing.

We are getting ready to put our house on the market, and already have our sights set on a lovely two-story on five acres west of our little town. With the kids' busy schedules and trying to get the house ready, I am more annoyed at having to fit yet another appointment into my calendar than I am about why I might need a repeat mammogram.

I make the appointment, and a few days later stand patiently while I have my breasts mashed under the compression paddle of a mammogram machine one more time. This time I am told to stay in the waiting room until the radiologist can look at my results. When I am called back to speak with the doctor, he shows me a black and white image on a screen and points to what he calls "areas of calcification." A biopsy will be needed to get a better idea of what this is.

Sigh. I'm still not worried, just annoyed. Who has time for this?

As time has passed, I have come to refer to my thirties as "The Clenched Years." Though filled with wonderful moments of taking the kids camping, laughing together (quietly, for Courtney's sake), of making lovely and hilarious family memories, it was a period of serious control issues for me. Part of it came with the territory, with the season of life I was in. But much of it was just me.

In the way that I loved order and organization, loved knowing what to expect–*needed* to know what to expect–I had become a Christian who found security in rules and righteous living. I was in awe of God's love for me, but I wanted to be *the very best* Christian for Him. I was hyperaware of where "the line" was–that fine line you cross when you are *bad* and stay obediently behind when you are *good*. The more I "did," the more tightly I drew the line around me, leaving little room for grace both for others and for myself.

I had thoughts about what everyone's life should look like; if I was completely honest, I thought everyone should be like me. Though I truly believed I was a humble sinner and was so thankful for God's grace, my heart was deceitful! I realize now what I couldn't see then: that I had become like the servant in Mathew 18:25-33, gratefully receiving God's grace for myself yet demanding perfection from others.

I knew the proverbs that said, "Many are the plans in a man's heart, but it is the Lord's purpose that prevails," (19:21 NIV) and "Trust in the Lord with all your heart and lean not on your own understanding. In all your ways acknowledge him, and he will make your paths straight." (3:5-6 NASB)

Why did I keep leaning on my own understanding? Why did I think my way was better, was the right way? Why did I feel such a need to control everything? Was I trying to guarantee certain outcomes? What made me think that was even possible?

Almost every day during this time I would pour out my heart to the Lord in my journals, confessing my failings and praying fervently and passionately for those around me. But in practical life I would continue to control and micromanage.

Dad's memorial service had been a beautiful rendering of a life lived well–humble yet faithful, authentic but grace -filled. Steadfast. I found myself becoming obsessed with what my own funeral would look like. What would I be remembered for? How would my own life be summed up in a eulogy?

After Audrey turned a year old, Jim and I together decided that our nest was full; with the extra challenge of a child with special needs we both had peace about our family being complete. But it was only about a year later when seeds began sprouting in my mind about adopting a child. After hearing the emotional testimony on a radio program of one family's adoption of a daughter from China, I became convinced God was telling me this was His plan for us. It seemed everywhere I turned I was seeing families with adopted Asian daughters. He even brought a name to mind while I was mowing the backyard one day–Selah Grace. This was the name we had chosen for a daughter if Levi had been a girl. Since we never used the name, I took it to mean God was saving it for our adopted daughter. Really, in my mind, there was no reason *not* to adopt. We had so much to offer!

In the fall of 2004 Jim and I attended a Williams Syndrome convention in Grand Rapids to learn more about what exactly we would be dealing with as Courtney grew older. She had just turned seven, and we were looking further down the road regarding her schooling and other issues. While the convention was informative and helpful, and not a little overwhelming, I made the mistake of bringing up my desire to adopt to Jim during a lunch break.

His reaction, which I initially took to be anger, was one of sadness and injury. He was definitely *not* feeling "led by God" to adopt another child. "I feel like our children and all the attention they need is becoming a wall between us," he said. He inferred from my desire to adopt that what I did *not* desire was any time alone with him in the future. *Ouch.*

Here again was an example that my faith, though strong, was sometimes an emotional and idealistic fairyland through which I blissfully galloped on my unicorn, assuming that Jim would dance right along beside me. Instead, his voice of practicality and his humanness brought me back to earth. I was disappointed but Jim was right, and deep down I knew it.

What was my real motivation to adopt? Was I once again taking something that I admired about my parents and upping it a notch? Did I think that somehow we would be better adoptive parents than they had been? Or was I trying to add one more A+ to my report card to show God how much I was doing for him?

Seeing our life with a clarity that I sometimes lacked, Jim knew we were stretched thin. And that our marriage was feeling the strain.

Although I flourished in the role of motherhood, I had less and less energy left over for "wifing." Jim's travel schedule didn't help. I dug down deep in my continuing Bible studies and, though I was learning so much, I found myself becoming more and more legalistic and judgmental. In my personal prayer time and in my journals, I repeatedly bemoaned my sins and expressed humble gratitude for God's grace. I happily went about serving others as much as I could, but in my heart I was not sharing that same grace with them. And this included Jim.

Though I accepted and eventually agreed with the decision not to pursue adoption, a voice in my head kept nagging that I should be doing something "more." I began to confuse this inner, critical voice with the voice of the Holy Spirit, believing that I was never doing–or being–enough. I could hear the words of one of my beloved church mamas reminding me, "That's not your Father's voice!" But the enemy had gained a foothold.

I think poor Jim felt the same way–nothing he did was good enough. I was holding him and others to unrealistic standards that I could not even meet myself.

Serving others really did bring me joy–it was a blessing to be a blessing. But part of me served with a mindset of performance, keeping tally marks on my mental scorecard. Even though I barely had time to turn around and the challenges of Courtney loomed in front of us, I still felt like I was falling short somewhere. I believed strongly that God deserved so much more–that somehow He was not receiving glory if I was not busy serving Him. I believed that my children were my mission field in this season, but I also thought that since I did not work outside the home, I should have all the time in the world to be "doing things for God." Funny, shouldn't those two be the same thing?

Oh, but I was good at putting on my church face for Sunday mornings, my outward actions exemplifying grace and kindness and smiles; but it was in the inner thoughts of my heart, the dark private corners, where I smirked disapprovingly. In my mind, I was everyone's mom, boss, Holy Spirit, jury, and judge. The only one I defended was myself.

It was emotionally and physically draining. And it was catching up with me.

Almost five years to the day from my dad's death, I am diagnosed with stage 2 breast cancer. After the biopsy shows a small cancerous tumor in my left breast, I have a lumpectomy followed by another surgery that reveals cancer in my lymph nodes. Together Jim and I decide that I will pursue chemo and radiation.

One day between my biopsy and lumpectomy, I take my mom on a drive to show her the new house we will soon be moving to. And I am forced to use the C-word once again in her presence.

"Oh, Cher," she says, laying her hand on my arm. I see tears in her eyes as I swipe at my own; the word *cancer* hangs in the air between us, and I know a range of emotions are running through us both.

Jim, as stunned as I by the diagnosis, has rallied to be my rock. We have not yet told the kids, but plan to once treatment details are finalized. We have an amazing church family who are already on their knees for us. And I have a God who has never left my side. My safety net is strong.

And yet telling my mom about this feels like opening a wound that has finally, slowly, begun to heal.

The new house sits on five acres out in the country, within the same school district but further out in the quiet. It currently sits empty, so Mom and I walk right through the grass that needs mowing to peer into the windows. We sigh at the enormous open kitchen, run our hands over the textured stone running up to the roof on the front of the house, and marvel at all the land. The back deck overlooks a wide-open space edged by gentle trees. There are hints of perennial flowers starting to bloom, and I see bluebirds and cardinals in the air. It is breathtaking here.

Unbidden, the question enters my mind, "Will I live in this house? Or will I die in this house?"

I had been completely blindsided by the cancer diagnosis. I had been doing everything right! Eating well, running; I felt so good! How could my body betray me like this? I had no family history of breast cancer. None.

How could God allow this to happen?

I was worried about my grieving mother. I had a daughter with Williams Syndrome struggling now to navigate middle school–a double whammy. Not to mention a teenage driver and two younger children who still needed me. Parenting was hard. And as with all marriages, ours needed attention. I would offer up my life, my cares, my people to God in a tearful prayer, only to wrap my fingers tightly around them once again the minute I said "Amen."

Yet I truly believed that I was walking in grace with Him, that I was surrendering my circumstances to Him on a daily, sometimes momentary, basis. Did my heart need more refining?

I was so, so tired of trying to keep it all together.

In August, as I watch yet another clump of my hair swirl down the shower drain, I realize it is time for one more haircut, this time a truly defining one. I have been dreading this day. The thought of losing my hair has kept me tossing and turning at night, convinced my pillow will hold enough hair to sew together a wig when I wake up in the morning.

When I come downstairs, I quietly ask Jim to go get his clippers, trying not to draw attention from the kids. He meets me out on the back deck, bringing a stool from the kitchen for me to sit on. After he fastens the plastic cape around my neck, I bow my head as the clippers turn on with a buzz.

Sigh. Seems like we've been here before. I wonder if he will give me a grape dum-dum sucker when we're done. I smile in spite of myself. I don't deserve this man, this one who has already shaved his own head in solidarity.

As Jim clicks off the clippers, I rub my hands over my roughly sheared head. I dread the thought of looking in the mirror.

Small piles of my brown hair lay on the deck of our new house, and Jim walks inside to get the broom. I wipe the tears from my cheeks, trying to stifle my sobs so that the kids won't hear.

Without my hair, what message is being sent now?

I force myself to pick up the hand mirror I brought out to the deck with me. My patchy dome makes me look like a concentration camp survivor, and I can barely stand to look at my reflection.

But as I lay the mirror on my lap and gaze out to the trees beyond our property, I wonder if this new "hairstyle" could be a message of mercy? A sign of a shaven life that can now be completely reliant on the grace of God, His work, His ways...instead of Cheryl's?

For years now I have been working so hard to prove to the Lord how much I love Him. But I have fallen into the trap of thinking my relationship with Him is more about what I do than Who He is. Walking with Christ is not made up of rules and regulations or checklists. It is a relationship, it is grace, and it is Jesus–Someone who loves me and ultimately longs for my good.

I realize now that surrendering to God's grace is a process, a continual refinement, not a "one and done." And each time I surrender, our relationship is strengthened.

I see that grace is sufficient because it is both soft *and* strong. It is law, but it is also spirit.

It is undeserved favor; it is getting what you don't deserve and not getting what you do.

It requires nothing of me. The minute I start thinking it does, it is no longer free; it is no longer God's best.

It is one step forward, two steps back. New mercies every morning.

It is a living hope in darkness, in grief, and in the middle of the unknown.

Grace is "Go and sin no more," "There is now no condemnation," and "I have overcome the world."

It is mercy over judgment, animal skins over nakedness, snow over sins of scarlet.

It is free will, but not willing that any should perish.

It is wrath against sin that equals love.

It is tears in a bottle, it is 'Jesus wept,' it is every tear wiped away.

It is eternity in the hearts of men who live in earthly tents.

It is a loving mother and a solid father; a gentle Lion and a mighty Lamb.

It feels like it's time to surrender once again my whole life wholeheartedly, completely unhindered, to this great grace.

For so long I thought I had to be the one to hold up the tent in the storm.

Yet God keeps showing me that there will be times when the wind will blow down my tent completely–and my Father will keep me safe.

His winds of grace are always blowing regardless of what I do, and whether they blow the tent down or fill the sails, I know I am not alone.

Jim comes back outside with the broom but sets it aside when he sees my tears. He pulls me close as the wind gently blows my hair off the deck and out onto the green grass.

EPILOGUE

But He said to me, "My grace is sufficient for you,
for my power is made perfect in weakness."
Therefore I will boast all the more gladly of my weaknesses,
so that the power of Christ may rest upon me.

2 Corinthians 12:9 ESV

Grace and gratitude go hand in hand.

The days after each chemo treatment were spent resting in my chair in the living room, watching the chickadees and goldfinches outside the window, Bible and journal open on my lap.

Each Scripture-filled card sent from a friend or loved one I devoured like daily bread that nourished my hurting body and soul.

I made myself look each day for three things to thank God for. I recorded them on paper so I would remember not the pain, discomfort, and fear of this season, but the gifts of grace.

Funny–when I looked for them, I found them. And I saw God's hand in them all. In realizing that I wouldn't ever be able to "pay God back" for saving me, I found joy and peace in cultivating gratitude instead.

In the spring of 2020, nine years cancer free and newly 50, I read through all my journals and saw even more gifts from God, a grace map in my memories. I began to string words together on paper, to comprehend how such an abstract concept –grace–could mean so much. I looked for, and found, the many times in my life where His grace had carried me, strengthened me, sufficed.

Over the course of the next few years this book was born, and God's grace has both filled me and floored me.

Jim and I just celebrated thirty years of marriage and our kids are grown and adulting; grace reminds me of when I was their age, and I am grateful. In a sweet, surprising twist, Jared and his wife Jenni have become foster parents. Levi and Audrey are in college pursuing their passions, and I hold them prayerfully yet loosely in my hands. They are His.

Plans for Courtney to move into semi-independent living in 2020 were put on hold due to the COVID-19 pandemic. On Memorial Day she collapsed in the kitchen while putting her dinner plate in the dishwasher, and the next day a pacemaker was inserted near her heart. She was just 22. Jim and I could not thank God enough that she was still living with us when this occurred. Since then, God has placed her in a living situation that is even better than what we had originally been working towards–more than we could ask or imagine. She is fiercely independent and woefully forgetful, but we are all happy.

My mom is healthy and thriving. Seven more Esper grandchildren have arrived since Dad's passing, and we all showered her with words of love when we marked her 75th birthday at Crystal Mountain. She continues to find purpose through sewing for others and currently has a side hustle selling tote bags to raise money for charity (see Appendix).

I miss my dad still. I miss his laughter, his plans and schemes and twinkling eyes. I miss his energy for helping others and his grateful heart. I miss his phone calls to say, "I just wanted to hear your voice, Cher." And I miss the rich, joyful union that was Dad and Mom together. I am forever grateful to God for allowing me any part of it.

The letter my dad wrote to me when I was 23 and miserable about not teaching after five and a half years of college was probably the most memorable gift he ever gave me. He could've gone so many directions in that moment, yet he chose to tell me he loved me and show me incredible, unconditional grace. Not only that, but he was a huge supporter of me as a stay-at-home mom, encouraging me always and showing respect for the job that it is. I think of his letter often as my now-adult children navigate their futures.

As of this writing, I have been cancer-free for over ten years. According to the plaque on the walls of the Cancer Center in Zion, Illinois, I am a survivor; my dad is not. I don't need a plaque to tell me that Dad is in the better position. But traveling the road of his cancer journey deeply impacted me, giving me perspective and courage when I faced my own.

In the end, it is all God's grace, and it is enough for me.

Appendix

Behold, I am doing a new thing;
now it springs forth,
do you not perceive it?
I will make a way in the wilderness and rivers in the desert.

Isaiah 43:19 ESV

March 25, 2021

Go and Do Likewise [1]

MICHIGAN RESIDENTS ARE MOTIVATED BY THE STORY OF THE GOOD SAMARITAN TO MAKE AND SELL PURSES TO RAISE FUNDS FOR SAMARITAN'S PURSE.

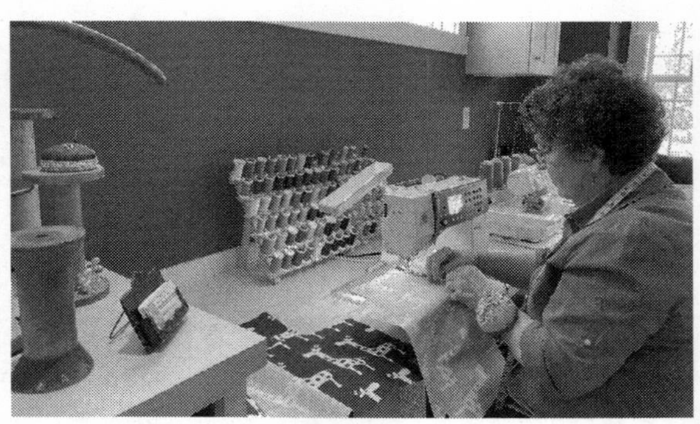

LYNDA ESPER SEWS PURSES AND TOTES TO "LET HER LIGHT SO SHINE BEFORE MEN" (MATTHEW 5:16).

A team of 11 women in the Holland, Michigan, area is tending to the needs of their "neighbors in a ditch" by stitching!

Over the past nine and a half years, the ladies have created over 6,000 purses and totes, giving all of the proceeds to Samaritan's Purse. The group, aptly called Purses for Samaritan's Purse, has raised $86,000 in donations for the ministry.

SOME OF THE PURSES FOR SAMARITAN'S PURSE PRODUCT

The group's founder, Lynda Esper, 74, was sitting at her sewing machine making a tote bag in 2011 when "the name just touched me," she said. "I believe it was from the Holy Spirit: Purses for Samaritan's Purse." Shortly afterward, Lynda sewed a large number of one-style totes and hosted an open house–and raised $300 from that first sale!

People soon began to hear about her endeavor, and other Christian women joined her in cutting fabric or sewing. Since they started nearly a decade ago, this team of retirees has expanded their product line to seven different styles of bags, ranging in price from $10 to $25.

"People will open up their home and invite their friends, but it's different [from other home parties] because we tell them what the purpose is," Lynda said.

A brochure about the worldwide relief-and-evangelism work of Samaritan's Purse goes inside every bag the group makes, and 100-percent of the purchase price goes to the ministry.

Supporting Work Done 'In Jesus' Name'

LYNDA'S CUTTERS AND SEWERS WORK TOGETHER TO CRAFT BEAUTIFUL HANDBAGS TO SELL.

The fact that everything at Samaritan's Purse is done in Jesus' Name is what first attracted Lynda to the organization. She learned of it while packing Operation Christmas Child gift-filled shoeboxes in 2008. When she traveled out of state to volunteer at a processing center, where shoeboxes are prepared for international shipment, she was impressed that "people prayed with you before you worked."

A couple years later when Purses for Samaritan's Purse was founded on the story of the Good Samaritan in Luke 10, Lynda felt that she could "go and do likewise" as the parable commands, by sewing. She chose Matthew 5:16 as a theme verse for the group: "Let your light so shine before men, that they may see your good works and glorify your Father in heaven." Lynda wants their work to shine before others in a way that will lead them to praise God. "It blesses me when people glorify God because of a little thing that I'm making."

Persnickety for a Purpose

Lynda purchases all of the supplies out of her own pocket and does so with great care. "I'm very persnickety, so I pick out the fabrics most of the time," she said. "The funny thing is, God has sent me very persnickety cutters and sewers."

THE PURSES FOR SAMARITAN'S PURSE TEAM IN MAY 2019 WITH THEIR FOUNDER LYNDA ESPER IN THE FRONT IN THE PINK JACKET.

The team's precise, careful approach to their work is an important quality, Lynda says. "We always get comments about how well the purses are made. I feel that everything we do is for God's glory, and we don't want to give Him anything but our best."

After she makes fabric selections, Lynda sends the material to the cutters, who follow plexiglass patterns with a rotary blade. They return the cut pieces to Lynda who assembles bundles of scissors, thread, fabric, and handles for each of the sewers.

Each volunteer serves independently on their own time, but the group gathers to celebrate together once or twice a year.

When the global pandemic limited open houses, the team shifted gears and made over 900 masks. The switch broadened their customer base to corporations. The companies then sent their donations directly to Samaritan's Purse.

'Liberated to Love Lavishly'

Somewhere over the years, Lynda picked up the life theme "because of Christ I am liberated to love lavishly." It's not unique to her, but she finds the phrase frees her from self-consciousness and sin. "He's overcome the world, so I can do what He told me to do: love Him and love others," Lynda said. "And it doesn't mean that every day is peachy keen."

LYNDA SELLS THE TOTES AT HOME PARTIES WHERE SHE CLEARLY STATES THE PURPOSE IS TO SUPPORT SAMARITAN'S PURSE.

Lynda knows that all too well. In 2005, she and her husband Frank moved to Zeeland, Michigan, and set up life in a new condo, only to have him pass away from cancer less than six months later. They'd been married nearly 38 years. Alone in a new city with few friends, Lynda, then 59, set out to try and find God's purpose for her in this new season of life.

"The first couple of years, I could hold onto God's hand and that's about all I could do," Lynda said.

But in 2007, Lynda put a business card up at the local fabric store to begin serving again as a seamstress, a job she held while her children were growing up. Four years later, Purses for Samaritan's Purse was born.

'Do Something for Someone Else'

Lynda's oldest daughter, Cheryl Balcom, sees how Purses for Samaritan's Purse is allowing her mother to live out advice she used to give her children.

"When I was younger my mom would always say to us kids, 'Whenever you're feeling down, the best thing to do is something for someone else.'"

"Whenever you're feeling down, the best thing to do is something for someone else."

Over the years as Lynda's family grew, whichever room happened to serve as her sewing room at the time often got converted into a bedroom–resulting in Lynda's sewing machine eventually finding a home in the hallway.

"We fell asleep at night to the sound of her sewing machine," Cheryl said.

And today, that skill her mom first developed when she was 11 years old is blessing others in new ways as she and her team of volunteers continue to create bags that are sold, not only in Michigan, but also in Arizona, Florida, Idaho, Maryland, Virginia, and even Germany.

"It is an amazing testimony of God's faithfulness," Cheryl said. "He's redeemed this very difficult time in my mom's life and brought something beautiful out of it."

[1]: *Samaritan's Purse*, Go and Do Likewise https://samaritanspurse.org/article/go-and-do-likewise/

Thank You

All my life I knew I had a story to share, but I assumed my family would just one day go through my journals to read it after I died. It wasn't until I turned 50 that I realized no one in the world has that kind of time. I learned that if I wanted to share my story, I would have to be intentional about putting it together.

As the words filled the page and the story began to form, I discovered that my story is not about me at all, it's about God. Therefore, to Him be all the glory and all my gratitude, amen.

There are many incredible people who supported me during this journey, and I would like to thank them too.

Thank you, Mom, for saving all the letters, emails, updates, and the black leather datebook of all the appointments and visits. Your meticulous organization lent so much to telling this story accurately. The conversations over coffee, over dinner, and over the phone were priceless. I hope that in some way they brought healing to you as they did to me. Thank you most of all for loving and caring for Dad for 38+ years and for being an example to me of a faithful servant of Christ–no matter the circumstances. I love you.

Thank you to my husband Jim for your patience, your encouragement, for making me laugh, and for making me better, always.

Thank you, Reneé, for being the other half of all my memories. And for letting me wear the good pair of dock-siders to work at McDonald's.

To my beautiful children: Jared (and Jenni!), Courtney, Levi, and Audrey–thank you for loving me, in spite of me.

Special thanks to Pat Coffey, Mike Pruis, Craig Sisson, John Glessner, and Bruce Meles for sharing your memories of Dad with me and with Mom, and for being such great friends to my parents. God bless you.

Thank you, Lorilee Craker, for your skillful editing and heartfelt empathy; I know you have walked this road of loss, too. To Ann Byle, proofreader extraordinaire, thank you. I am also grateful for Autograph.pub for their help with the formatting of this book. And a heartfelt thank you to Jessie Clemence, whose initial encouragement humbled me, and confirmed I needed to keep writing.

And most of all, thank you Jesus for grace that I will never fully comprehend, but will always gratefully receive.

About the Author

Cheryl Esper Balcom is a reader and writer who recognized God's incredible faithfulness and sufficient grace in the pages of her personal journals, confirming all that she has learned from His word. She continues to write to encourage others to find that grace in their own lives. She and her husband Jim live on five acres tucked in the southwest corner of Michigan and love to spot wildlife out the window. They also enjoy camping and hiking together, as long as Jim carries the backpack.

Follow her on social media:
Facebook @cherylesperbalcom, writer
Instagram @cherylesperbalcom
To read more from Cheryl and to see additional photos from this story, visit: www.cherylesperbalcom.com

Made in the USA
Middletown, DE
11 February 2024